Perception is the Commodity

Manuscript by Sayyar Isma'il Swift

إن الحمد لله نحمده و نستعينه و نستغفره و نعود بالله من شرور انفسنا و
من سيئات أعمالنا من يهده الله فلا مضل له و من يضلل فلا هادي له و اشهد
أن لا إله إلا الله وحده لا شريك له و ان محمدا عبده و رسوله

يَاأَيِّهَا الَّذِينَ أمنُوا اتَّقوا اللَّه وَقولُوا قَوْلًا سِديدًا يُصلِحْ لَكُمْ أَعمالَكُمْ وَيَغْفِرْلَكُمْ
ذُنوبكُمْ وَمنْ يطِعِ اللَّه ورَسولَهُ فَقَدْ فازَ فَوْزًا عظِيما

All thanks and praise is due to Allah, we seek his help and forgiveness. We seek refuge in Allah from the evil within ourselves and the consequences of our evil deed. Whoever Allah guides will never be led astray, and whoever Allah leads astray will never find guidance. I bear witness there is no God but Allah, alone without partners and alone is his worship; I also bear witness that Muhammad s.a.w. is his last prophet, slave & Messenger...

Allah the exalted said, "O you who have believed, fear Allah as he should be feared and speak words of appropriate justice, he will then amend your deeds and forgive you your sins, and whoever obeys Allah and his messenger has certainly attained a great attainment" [33:70-71]

A student of knowledge I love to share new insights & understandings to open the minds of others. The world we live in has progressively worsened due to our own degrading levels. Therefore it will only be corrected by holding ourselves accountable accordingly. Writing is something I find to be a form of further study & research. In' Sha Allah, I will enable myself and others towards a better direction and future outcome.

So, by Allah my creator and sustainer I hope to share in an effort of benefiting those who read with increased awareness & insight that will enable us all in helping one another see and avoid societal engineered traps that aim at re-writing the human being...

Nathartukum elay Al-Tarwati

Perception is the Commodity

Psychological look into the conformity of society...

By

Sayyar Isma'il Swift

[Student of knowledge/Psychology Major]

Compiled in Morocco 2016 ©

Edited by:

Cover Art work: Sayyar Isma'il Swift

ISLAMIC REFERENCES TAKEN FROM QURAN AND SUNNAH OF THE
PROPHET MUHAMMAD S.A.W IN AUTHENTIC, SAHIH CLASSED AHADITH,
OF THE MAJOR COMPILERS OF HADITH.

Table of Contents

Preface

There are a number of reasons that contribute to the sublime ideals behind why we do what we do, however there are along with our own drives other engineered incentives that further stir us to behavior not derived from ourselves. As mankind becomes more and more duped away from purpose and his/her own higher purpose, we become more susceptible to the coercions that are aligned at detouring us towards artificial means. So subtle, the likeness of television commercials, all have undertones that play to the human psyche that psychologist and others who have employed them in gaining this understanding in order to exploit and help them in their plans of control; implementing these subliminal measures into every facet of life until society is completely enveloped and thus manipulated...

Have you ever wonder why they are so many psychological distractions today? Television is interrupted with commercials, public transportation, park benches; sides of public structures all consistently displaying signage & advertisement that flood the mental intake of a person. These apparatuses of deliberate distraction are prevalent in the urban areas, while suburban and other areas are more peaceful and calm because the mind is more so able to relax because there is less mental stimulus bombarding the person.

This of course varies from one society to another, and also may be biased to ethnicity, culture, and other norms that are understood in those societies. Well understood psychological instruments that have been developed know that with cultural differences there will be shifts to the societal norms. Therefore, other means will have to be designed to target the norms of those different cultures...In my opinion this is where American pop-culture and its export and influence help to bridge the gap of understanding the differences between cultures as well as offering insight into how better to target their interest. Because much can be lost in the potency of a message in translation, language instruments have to be developed in order to have the same effects as those of the original target language. In turn, we should understand the importance of the celebrity that is paired with his or her influence and the tactfully employed deception of engineering societal change, in which they are paid vast amounts...

Foreword

"Some of the biggest men in the United States, in the field of Commerce & Manufacturing, are afraid of somebody, are afraid of something...They know that there is a power somewhere so organized, so subtle, so watchful, so interlocked, so complete, so pervasive that they had better not speak above their breath when they speak in condemnation of it."

[President Woodrow Wilson] In his book "THE NEW FREEDOM", published in 1913

The world has repeated in cylindrical fashion back to the ways of tyrants who deem themselves superior and commit the same lude acts {shirk, association of partners & themselves with the Most High} as those who have preceded them...Fearing NOT the moment of death by constant denial with arrogant ideas of long life, and splendor that keeps them safe from a day in which they will return to Allah... corruption is rooted in their thoughts of being blessed with material gain, but instead it is their portion given to them in this world at the loss of the eternal as they only become more extravagant in mischief & waste...

وَقَالَ مُوسَى رَبَّنَا إِنَّكَ آتَيْتَ فِرْعَوْنَ وَمَلَأَهُ زِينَةً وَأَمْوَالًا فِي الْحَيَاةِ الدُّنْيَا رَبَّنَا لِيُضِلُّوا عَن سَبِيلِكَ ۖ رَبَّنَا اطْمِسْ عَلَى أَمْوَالِهِمْ وَاشْدُدْ عَلَى قُلُوبِهِمْ فَلَا يُؤْمِنُوا حَتَّى يَرَوُا الْعَذَابَ الْأَلِيمَ

And Moses said, "Our Lord, indeed You have given Pharaoh and his establishment splendor and wealth in the worldly life, our Lord, that they may lead [men] astray from Your way. Our Lord, obliterate their wealth and harden their hearts so that they will not believe until they see the painful punishment." [Yunus 10:88]

قَالَ قَدْ أُجِيبَت دَّعْوَتُكُمَا فَاسْتَقِيمَا وَلَا تَتَّبِعَانِّ سَبِيلَ الَّذِينَ لَا يَعْلَمُونَ

[Allah] said, "Your supplication has been answered." So remain on a right course and follow not the way of those who do not know."[Yunus 10:89]

وَجَاوَزْنَا بِبَنِي إِسْرَائِيلَ الْبَحْرَ فَأَتْبَعَهُمْ فِرْعَوْنُ وَجُنُودُهُ بَغْيًا وَعَدْوًا ۖ حَتَّى إِذَا أَدْرَكَهُ الْغَرَقُ قَالَ آمَنتُ أَنَّهُ لَا إِلَهَ إِلَّا الَّذِي آمَنَتْ بِهِ بَنُو إِسْرَائِيلَ وَأَنَا مِنَ الْمُسْلِمِينَ

And We took the Children of Israel across the sea, and Pharaoh and his soldiers pursued them in tyranny and enmity until, when drowning overtook him, he said, "I believe that there is no deity except that in whom the Children of Israel believe, and I am of the Muslims."{those who submit} [Yunus 10:90]

آلْآنَ وَقَدْ عَصَيْتَ قَبْلُ وَكُنتَ مِنَ الْمُفْسِدِينَ

Now?{Allah says} And you had disobeyed [Him{Musa's prophet-hood}] before and were of the corrupters? [Yunus 10:91]

Public relations and its concepts of control have primitive roots. In situations often people lacked the sense of personal identity as do people today in contemporary times, which has always made it ease for rulers to fill that void. Resources of taboos, super-naturalism, and force were a means of gathering the attentions of following subjects. Upon amassing more control and influence came the conditions by which wealth was grown & harvested that helped to build into the grandeur of the ruler altering further the psyche of the subjects. Wealth is the means by which people are most prone to manipulation and corrupted by its fleeting allure from personal grasp and settling illusion upon those who have gained through manipulation; misleading the weak into further deviance. As in the story of Musa a.s. and the wealth of Firaun. Power to mislead is therefore power to control, so if one isn't able to mislead or influence the people then one's power will fade...

The vast personal wealth of Firaun wasn't holistically hinged on the abilities of his person, but it is in fact part & parcel of the control he had over is people through myth of being god on earth to his own people and his subjugation of power on Banu Israel {children of Israel}. The similarities have been true with colonialization, slavery and also with stories even today with some Kings claiming lineage back to the Prophet Muhammad s.a.w. in an effort to solidify their succession in rule with divine legitimacy. Only fools buy into the myth, for if that were true their rule should model the divine legitimacy they claim...

Through his wealth {Firaun=Pharaoh} he was able to maintain this fiction with the best of methods and strategies that were in opposition to the prophet-hood of Musa a.s & Harun a.s. (Moses and Aaron).
Turning repeatedly from the warnings & signs of the true reality that would surely seal his fate witnessing miracle after miracle un-humbled until he was on the verge of dealth..The Quran today house the auditory miracles of Allah in ultimate truth which is explaining the world in which we live from the time it was revealed {succeeding the previous books} until the last day. So, Again Firaun is in denial of the many signs that are being shown him, predicting our anticipation to the repeated fate(s) of those prior.

Once again the days of extravagance are dwindling to and end as their appointed term come to a close. Awakening the people towards truth... Struggles, patient and faithful the restoration of justice will return as promised to lead the people aright again freeing us from the tyranny of those who misuse power for corruption & sin. However, freedom won't come without Firaun giving chase once again ...not readily willing to relinquish his power he still seeks to manipulate and enslave the people anyway he can. Fiat currency will collapse but in the meantime capturing as many new debt-slaves as possible along with psychological manipulation to further confuse and eradicated faith from society altogether towards a New Satanic principal.
Already in full of understanding of their own mortality & false self-image, it will only be death that kills their disease of arrogance.

It seems that many former-presidents knew of this invisible organization that keeps to the shadows in manipulating the rule of governments, business, war, and society as a whole...Its been called many things such as the Military industrial Complex by former President Dwight Eisenhower while just alluded too by others to their existence...

The following speech by one of the most famous U.S. Presidents' to date still resonates in my mind especially the portion I'm highlighting for you from his speech that addresses the matter. What the then President was saying as well as others before him, were in fact warning the population of pending dangers that had long been enacted into these covert tactics against the people. However, it seems as though many didn't hear the words or better yet, didn't understand what they were trying to warn the people against. It's a well-known fact that the cognitive abilities of people who subdue themselves in distractions that are misleading in or of themselves will often fail to understand the intangible world & the hidden principals that target humanities higher purpose...

*The very word **"secrecy"** is repugnant in a free and open society; and we are as a people inherently and historically opposed to secret societies, to secret oaths and to secret proceedings;*

*Even today, there is little value in opposing the threat of a closed society by **imitating its arbitrary restrictions**. Even today, there is little value in insuring the survival of our nation if our traditions do not survive with it. {The traditions by which the Nation was founded, although constricted to more racial bias, the founding documents that were meant to be living-documents; were full of just measures to protect the society}*

***Our way of life is under attack {freedoms}.** Those who make themselves our enemy are advancing around the globe. The survival of our friends is in danger. **And yet no war has been declared, no borders have been crossed by marching troops, no missiles have been fired.** {Because this war is psychological}*

*I can only say that **no war ever posed a greater threat** to our security...{to humanity}*

***It requires a change in outlook**, a change in tactics, a change in missions—by the government, **by the people**, by every businessman or labor leader, and by every newspaper. For we are opposed around the world by a **monolithic {which means it's a single organization}** and ruthless conspiracy that **relies primarily on covert means** for expanding its sphere of influence—**on infiltration instead of invasion, on subversion instead of elections, on intimidation instead of free choice, on guerrillas by night instead of armies by day**. It is a system which has conscripted {Read the writing of Albert Pike who outline the methods they have followed} vast human and material resources into the building of a tightly knit, highly efficient machine that combines **military, diplomatic, intelligence, economic, scientific and political operations**...*

Its preparations are concealed, not published. Its mistakes are buried, not headlined. Its dissenters are silenced {means killed}, not praised. No expenditure is questioned, no rumor is printed, and no Secret is revealed. It conducts the Cold War; in short, with a war-time discipline no democracy would ever hope or wish to match...

[President John F. Kennedy] *Address before the American Newspaper Publishers Association, April 27, 1961 two years later November 22, 1963 he was assassinated...*

History polled against its own understanding with the conclusion of events that shift society towards the pre-conceived ideals that are being covertly driven towards. When society resist, it causes setbacks in their efforts; but when society conforms they gain

more ground & with that more control over every aspect of life...

Perception is the Commodity, so Why do we Conform?

Being Human

Like the computer the human brain inputs, processes, stores and outputs information in the form of actions & behavior. Although our societies have evolved in the since & use of technology, the question is debatable over how much have our brains evolved? In terms of usage & cognitive abilities that develop pre-natal through puberty. Studies have shown that usage to be far less than preceding generations; most notably paired with technological advancement only, the usage of our brains has suffered greatly as people become more so dependent on the use of technology.

Computers resemble the human body in many ways, which gives it orientation & reference to its own design & sophistication. But, there are still some significant differences that we have over the computer.

- Information processing for human being is done through the Central Nervous System where the Computer has a distributed type of processing that requires prioritizing of importance.
- Data input for the human is parallel, simultaneous and sometimes even subconscious where the computer is sequential logic.
- Output for the human being is overlaid onto personal drives, motives, experience, etc. where the computer would be Exclusive and limited to a cause & effect type behavior acting on what was inputed.
- Storage for the human would be the connections made in the brain and the computer is limited to addressing
- Initiation for the human is cognitive (& spiritual driven) as for the computer it would be solely input driven. The absence of input would be the absence of initiation...

These differences are substantial in ability and design primarily because of our spiritual and biological anatomy and blessing from the creator. However, what happens to the Human being as he/she begins to forfeit those cognitive abilities to inanimate objects of dependency? Now, the differences began to take on new meaning and narrow the gap between human & machine. Psychology is only about 100 yrs. old in the sense of a formal science although many people through spiritual study, curiosity and knowledge of scripture & prophetic teaching all tapped into this understanding long ago. From a Western point of view taking their understanding back to the Greeks in the 3rd and 4th centuries this then explored idea was brought about to better understand the distinction between the living and the dead, Ideas to understanding the heart & emotion, rationalism and deductive reasoning something that Socrates, Plato & Aristotle are referenced for. It wasn't until the 19th century that scientific psychology by William James arose with the advent of World Wars where intelligence testing began to be used in order to group people based on intellect. Intellectual ability was therefore used in personnel placement of people into society. This particular parcel is still in use today by the United States Armed Forces in their entry examination (ASVAB). The score of the applicant is overlaid with corresponding jobs that will be referred to the individual thus placing them accordingly within their Military society where that person is perceived best suitable. Like many early works, what they lack in total understanding, prejudices, and other biases; it still provides a platform on which later work can continue to build upon. Ultimately, as more understanding came about it would only be the applications of those understandings that would stand in the way of higher praise.

Hence with these deeper insights came their employment into the manipulation & control of Human being. With systematic approaches of analysis & understanding that helps to predict the behavior of the human being other measure could then be interjected into society at their behest. For example, Today science know from understanding the importance of breast feeding is a very critical precursor to proper child development [Quran 2:233], as are other physical development related items such as Nutrition. Alterations of breast feeding to formulas as rob children of a crucial bond with the mother of wet nurse that has been proven to psychologically effect the child in brain development. In addition to that is the broken family or two-parent working families that further this decadence. This has then opened the door to genetically altered foods which affect physical and mental development further into puberty and beyond. Also the harmful effects on the mother...Breast cancer has lower probability on breast feeding mothers and the more times (multiple births) she has breast fed further reduces that risk. Furthermore the uterine involution of the uterus retracting from a pregnant state back to a non-pregnant state is also linked to breastfeeding. The chemical Oxytocin is released from breastfeeding as well as Prolactin which aids this process. No one would suspect such a deep impact on society from a responsibility of the mother to her child in neglect or deviance due to societal influences that make women not perform this duty.

Traditional Classroom	Constructivist Classroom
Curriculum begins with the parts of the whole. Emphasizes basic skills.	Curriculum emphasizes big concepts, beginning with the whole and expanding to include the parts.
Strict adherence to fixed curriculum is highly valued.	Pursuit of student questions and interests is valued.
Materials are primarily textbooks and workbooks.	Materials include primary sources of material and manipulative materials.
Learning is based on repetition.	Learning is interactive, building on what the student already knows.
Teachers disseminate information to students; students are recipients of knowledge.	Teachers have a dialogue with students, helping students construct their own knowledge.
Teacher's role is directive, rooted in authority.	Teacher's role is interactive, rooted in negotiation.
Assessment is through testing, correct answers.	Assessment includes student works, observations, and points of view, as well as tests. Process is as important as product.
Knowledge is seen as inert.	Knowledge is seen as dynamic, ever changing with our experiences.
Students work primarily alone.	Students work primarily in groups.

Figure 1 Piaget's Classroom Model to Cognitive development

Woman and their protection now take on new and prolific meaning to preserve the individual, the family, education, and society. In the figurative sense of direct interference or alteration of this completely over looked phenomenon they are literally able to proportionately affect the psychological & develop status of an individual...

Narrated by Abu Umanmah al-Bahili

The prophet s.a.w. said: while I was sleep, two men (angels) came to me, held my upper arms, and took me to a rough mountain. They said, "Climb." I said, "I cannot climb it." They said, "We will make it easy for you." He continued: "So I ascended until I reached a high place in the mountain. I heard fierce cries and asked, "What are those cries?" They replied, "That is the howling of the people of the fire." He continued: "We moved on until I saw some people who were suspended by their Achilles tendon, their cheeks cut and gushing blood. I asked, "Who are those?" They replied, "Those are the ones who break their fast when it is not permissible." He continued: "We moved on until I saw people who were awfully swollen, and had the most foul stench and the most hideous appearance. I asked, "Who are those?" He replied, "Those are the dead of the kufar (on the battlefield)." He continued: "We moved on until I saw some people who were awfully swollen, and had the most foul stench—their stench was like that of the gutters. I asked, "Who are those?" They replied, "Those are the male-female adulterers." He continued: "We moved on until I saw some women with snake biting at their breast. I asked, "Who are those?" They replied, "Those are the women who deny their children their milk." He continued: "We moved on until I saw boys playing between two rivers. I asked, "Who are those?" They replied, "Those are the believer offspring (who died before puberty.)

-Verified Sahih by Sheikh Albani rahimullah alayhu

This hadith of the prophet s.a.w who was shown some of the punishments that will take place in the hell fire and their causes points to the importance of breastfeeding & is punishment for neglect. I would like to point out that some might think in opposition or in extreme to what is read, but on the contrary of personal emotion we must understand the generation impact that one mother can have on a society. If that is multiplied by 10,100,or 1000's of mothers then what we have then is a non-existing functional society that is full of psychological problems as well as under developed...

In the previous figure we can see the contrast between traditional classrooms and that considered to be more constructive for students. Its apparent that the current education system benefits those who have power in maintaining that power. Big concepts beginning with the whole and expanding to include the different parts is something I have always considered with regard to the problems we have consecutively faced year after year...Instead of seeing things from the nation-state perspective, it is now incumbent upon humanity to consider itself and its problems as a whole. Because, despite what one is able to physically see or not see, doesn't mean that there isn't a problem (*out of sight out of mind*). The world has come into focus, literally in the hands & pockets of millions with the ability to access or send information around the world in an instant. Our lives overlap, and our actions and economies overlap...thus the suffering of people elsewhere in the world is often the direct result of another's policies. I have shared previously the idea of America's greed and consumption being literally the driving force behind her foreign policy, and by that countries that are usurped for cheap labor and natural resources are held in weakened financial states provoking impoverished conditions while higher tiered countries exploit their gains in profit. How is it then that much of the world overlooks this reality which isn't hard at all to understand???

Cognitive Development (brief)

Piaget (1936) was a Swiss developmental psychologist known for his studies in children focusing on how they develop which enabled him to draft one of the most elaborate theories about the development process of cognition. Piaget described his work as genetic epistemology (*i.e. the origins of thinking*). Genetics is the scientific study of where things come from (*their origins*). Epistemology is concerned with the basic categories of thinking, that is to say, the framework or structural properties of intelligence. What sets his theory apart from others is the fact that it is based on observation more so than theoretical. This of course leverages his theories on solid evidence unlike hunches of others. The common assumption in psychology was that children are merely less competent thinkers than adults. One criticism is he claimed human beings to have a clean slate of intelligence when born, something that opposed others such as Lev Vygotsky, a Russian researcher in the same field. He claimed that humans are not born completely free of intelligence, for smell, taste, touch are present at birth with sight coming about 1wk later or so. What this means is we are born with natural instincts which harbor intelligence. For example a baby is able to recognize his/her mother smell & voice, that recognition is enabled by intelligence which is something that agrees with al-fitrah (the natural disposition) of the human being.

Abu Huraira (ra) reported: that the Prophet Muhammad (saw) said: "No one is born except they are upon natural instinct (fitrah); then his parents turn him/her into a Jew, Christian or Magian; as animals produce their young with perfect limbs, do you see anything defective?" Then Abu Huraira (ra) said, "Recite the verse if you wish," "So direct your face toward the religion, inclining towards truth; the nature of Allah upon which he has created the people." "No change should there be in the creation of Allah, that is the correct religion, but most of the people do not know." [Sahih Muslim, book 33 number 6423].

So, because of these innate senses of intelligence it is thus heavily important the acquisition of language, which he Vygotsky said is one of the most important criteria to development beyond the scope of our sensory intelligence of instinct. Confirmation of the importance of language for further development to function in this world is mentioned in the Quran with the story of Adam who was created "ON THE IMAGE" of a man already, not having to grow up from infancy to adolescence to adulthood because he had no parents: وَعَلَّمَ آدَمَ الْأَسْمَاءَ كُلَّهَا ثُمَّ عَرَضَهُمْ عَلَى الْمَلَائِكَةِ فَقَالَ أَنبِئُونِي بِأَسْمَاءِ هَٰؤُلَاءِ إِن كُنتُمْ صَادِقِينَ And He taught Adam the names - all of them. Then He showed them to the angels and said, "Inform Me of the names of these, if you are truthful." [Al-Baqarah 2:31] قَالُوا سُبْحَانَكَ لَا عِلْمَ لَنَا إِلَّا مَا عَلَّمْتَنَا ۖ إِنَّكَ أَنتَ الْعَلِيمُ الْحَكِيمُ They said, "Exalted are You; we have no knowledge except what You have taught us. Indeed, it is you who is the Knowing, the Wise." [Al-Baqarah 2:32] قَالَ يَا آدَمُ أَنبِئْهُم بِأَسْمَائِهِمْ ۖ فَلَمَّا أَنبَأَهُم بِأَسْمَائِهِمْ قَالَ أَلَمْ أَقُل لَّكُمْ إِنِّي أَعْلَمُ غَيْبَ السَّمَاوَاتِ وَالْأَرْضِ وَأَعْلَمُ مَا تُبْدُونَ وَمَا كُنتُمْ تَكْتُمُونَ He said, "O Adam, inform them of their names." And when he had informed them of their names, He said, "Did I not tell you that I know the unseen [aspects] of the heavens and the earth? And I know what you reveal and what you have concealed." [Al-Baqarah 2:33].

Further on Allah mentions some of his signs to humanity: وَمِنْ آيَاتِهِ خَلْقُ السَّمَاوَاتِ وَالْأَرْضِ وَاخْتِلَافُ أَلْسِنَتِكُمْ وَأَلْوَانِكُمْ ۚ إِنَّ فِي ذَٰلِكَ لَآيَاتٍ لِّلْعَالِمِينَ And of His signs is the creation of the heavens and the earth and the diversity of your languages and your colors. Indeed in that are signs for those of knowledge. [Ar-Rum 30:22]. In addition to human beings the gift of language transcends into the animal kingdom and that of creation itself. اصْبِرْ عَلَىٰ مَا يَقُولُونَ وَاذْكُرْ عَبْدَنَا دَاوُودَ ذَا الْأَيْدِ ۖ إِنَّهُ أَوَّابٌ

Be patient over what they say and remember Our servants, David, the possessor of strength; indeed, he was one who repeatedly turned back [to Allah]. [As'Sad 38:17]

إِنَّا سَخَّرْنَا الْجِبَالَ مَعَهُ يُسَبِّحْنَ بِالْعَشِيِّ وَالْإِشْرَاقِ Indeed, We subjected the mountains [to praise] with him, exalting [Allah] in the [late] afternoon and [after] sunrise. [As'Sad 38:18]

وَالطَّيْرَ مَحْشُورَةً ۖ كُلٌّ لَّهُ أَوَّابٌ

And the birds were assembled, all with him repeating [praises]. [As'Sad 39:19] وَشَدَدْنَا مُلْكَهُ وَآتَيْنَاهُ الْحِكْمَةَ وَفَصْلَ الْخِطَابِ And We strengthened his kingdom and gave him wisdom and discernment in speech. [As'Sad 38:20].

وَوَرِثَ سُلَيْمَانُ دَاوُودَ ۖ وَقَالَ يَا أَيُّهَا النَّاسُ عُلِّمْنَا مَنطِقَ الطَّيْرِ وَأُوتِينَا مِن كُلِّ شَيْءٍ ۖ إِنَّ هَٰذَا لَهُوَ الْفَضْلُ الْمُبِينُ

And Solomon inherited David. He said, "O people, we have been taught the language of birds, and we have been given from all things. Indeed, this is evident bounty." [An-Naml 27:16] وَحُشِرَ

لِسُلَيْمَانَ جُنُودُهُ مِنَ الْجِنِّ وَالْإِنسِ وَالطَّيْرِ فَهُمْ يُوزَعُونَ
And gathered for Solomon were his soldiers of the jinn and men and birds, and they were [marching] in rows. [An-Naml 27:17]

حَتَّى إِذَا أَتَوْا عَلَى وَادِ النَّمْلِ قَالَتْ نَمْلَةٌ يَا أَيُّهَا النَّمْلُ ادْخُلُوا مَسَاكِنَكُمْ لَا يَحْطِمَنَّكُمْ سُلَيْمَانُ وَجُنُودُهُ وَهُمْ لَا يَشْعُرُونَ

Until, when they came upon the valley of the ants, an ant said, "O ants, enter your dwellings that you not be crushed by Solomon and his soldiers while they perceive not." [An-Naml 27:18]

فَتَبَسَّمَ ضَاحِكًا مِّن قَوْلِهَا وَقَالَ رَبِّ أَوْزِعْنِي أَنْ أَشْكُرَ نِعْمَتَكَ الَّتِي أَنْعَمْتَ عَلَيَّ وَعَلَى وَالِدَيَّ وَأَنْ أَعْمَلَ صَالِحًا تَرْضَاهُ وَأَدْخِلْنِي بِرَحْمَتِكَ فِي عِبَادِكَ الصَّالِحِينَ

So [Solomon] smiled, amused at her speech {the ant}, and said, "My Lord, enable me to be grateful for Your favor which You have bestowed upon me and upon my parents and to do righteousness of which You approve. And admit me by Your mercy into [the ranks of] Your righteous servants."[An-Naml 27:19].

Science today has in fact paid close attention to communication among ants because of the extraordinary abilities to work together cohesively to accomplish very impressive feats. This evidence of science conforming to what was already understood through scripture 14 centuries ago provides further evidence against the notion of evolution. In fact language is one of "THE" best proofs that refute evolution. Noam Chomsky, famous professor of M.I.T. conducted an experiment with a chimpanzee they named "Nim." They began with sign language exactly the way that a child is taught regular language with use of flash cards with photos etc. Nim would later be able to request bananas or other simple sentences; however he sentences would not be grammatically correct. Word grouping such as: Drink me Nim, Eat me Nim, banana me Nim me...In addition prime mates don't have the same phonetic apparatus or vocal cords as do human, which led them to sign-language in the first place. The experiment proved that no language in the same since of human do they have, but animals more so use a code to communicate. (**Monferrato, 2015**)

Language is still something that either educates or is used in ways of misapplication, and distortion that continue to teach society often upon the misuse of words or phrases especially in accordance to Arabic & Islam as we see in media use today. I myself have tried explaining on many occasions the need of understanding the usage of language & laws even in translation. This is largely the primary reason many non-Semitic speakers (Most Christians) misinterpret the bible. Language development is made of 4 main skills which would also apply to understanding new language.

1. Phonology: involves the rules about the structure and sequence of speech sounds.
2. Semantics: consists of vocabulary and how concepts are expressed through words.
3. Grammar: involves two parts. The first, Syntax is the rules in which words are arranged into sentences. Second, morphology is the use of grammatical markers (indicating tense, active or passive voice etc.)
4. Pragmatics: the rules for appropriate and effective communication. Pragmatics involves 3 skills: using language for different purposes, changing language for

talking differently depending on whom it is you are talking to, and following rules such as turn taking and staying on topic. (**Monferrato, 2015**)

Yet, by 4mos of age, children are able to discriminate between speeches and sounds engaging in their own forms of babbling. Researches further suggest that the earliest acquisition of language begins in the uterus when the foetus begins to recognize the patterns & sounds of the mother voice. Ironically this particular proof happens to coincide with a story I heard about a mother who was memorizing the Quran. While she was pregnant the mother was working to memorize a significant portion of the Quran, reciting herself and listening during the entire time of the pregnancy. After giving birth and the child grew, she enrolled the child into the class for memorization of Quran. The teacher noticed that the child was whizzing through the pages very easy, so when the parents asked about the child's progress he was utterly amazed. He explained how well the child was performing, moving along very quickly. The mother asked what section they were in, and the teacher informed them. She smiled when she heard the teacher tell them the portion of the Quran they were in…The teacher, puzzled says, "What is it?" She replies, "This is the same portion of the Quran I was memorizing while I was pregnant with him/her." So, there seems to be some significance to the research.

Despite some small overlooking of consideration into his theory, Piaget was still able to show that young children think in strikingly different ways compared to adults (**McLeod, 2009**). According to Piaget schemas are a mental framework that allows us to take shortcuts in interpreting information. This is both the category of acquisition & processing of knowledge. Experiences occur delivering new information (new schema) which in turn modifies or changes altogether that schema that was before prevalent. A sort of re-writing of a mental law from one found to take higher precedence. As children these formalities create within our brains connections that have been discovered during the middle and late childhood with most of the changes occurring in the pre-frontal cortex. This area of the brain is a crucial area for many tasks while we are still children and not yet able to do. Studies further suggest that the overall thickness of the cerebral cortex is responsible for language, learning, reading & writing. This is the reasoning behind optimal stimulation of infants in regards to the connections that are then formed by these first experiences of learning within our environments. Assimilations which are the incorporating of new information into the bank of existing schemas; these help to fill in the gaps of pre-existing beliefs or understandings… For example: When a child sees a picture of an apple he or she is only familiar with the photo description of an apple. This may include the various colors & shape but it doesn't include the further descriptions of texture, smell or taste until the child actually comes into contact with an apple. If blind folded and given a piece to eat the child wouldn't know what he/she is eating, so this assimilation is needed to complete the pre-existing understanding. Accommodation is another gap filler in the sense that it also helps with distinctions. For example all four legged animals aren't dogs enabling more understanding. Finally, there's equilibration.

Piaget believed that all children try to strike a balance between assimilation & accommodation to achieve the mechanism of equilibration. Previous knowledge of assimilation is balance with new knowledge of accommodation through changing behavior. This process he explained was that giving ability to children to move from one stage to into the next... (Monferrato, 2015)

On the dark side of the coin, all of this studied information has proven useful in a beneficial manner as well as negative ways. Its advantageous for better nurturing these early years of development in order to raise more cognitive efficient people; however when applied tactfully for control it under minds society as a whole depriving us of more suitable means & higher standards of living. When psychology turns from medicine to weapon the implications are far reaching into the future with the ability to effect succeeding generations. Political measures enforced upon the education systems are deliberately targeted & used against humanity in making the human being less human & more so like machines that can be programmed to blindly follow and initiated through psychological means triggered by sound, sight or cathartic episodes for emotional response. Behaviors are modified accordingly from far more media exposure to later generations, which is an indication of cognitive restructuring. What that means is people no longer think, believe or process information in the same way; much like having a new computer code overwrite an existing one...the previous functions are obsolete & the new program becomes the primary source of its processing, so the external behavior is varied greatly as a consequence. In essence a new reality has been created...

Conformity

Whenever we change our behavior, views, and attitudes in response to the real or imagined presence of others, we are experiencing conformity. Although brief & touching on some key underlying assessments all important to our development actually determine our later abilities in life as adults. Everything we find present in the world is here for our use, but that usage should be in line with correct morals, values and attitudes. Education, and the nurturing of children towards progressive development lays the foundation of critical thinking & positive reactionary adults that will impact our society in ways that will cultivate life with enhancements that aren't illusionary toward materialism only but beneficial in the real sense of our purpose in this life. Teaching children to be bold in confidence, holding a capacity of goodness for others in high regard, to being self-disciplined when angry with sound moral behaviour that isn't hasty nor done without thought all ensure to have children who have personalities that are well balanced. Something else that should be done is removing fear, shyness, inferiority complexes, envy and anger...these characteristics can be seen as early as 4 months witnessing the child turning away his/her head when spoken too. An early example in the time of the prophet s.a.w. was that of Ibn Umar (ra)...

حَدَّثَنَا قُتَيْبَةُ، حَدَّثَنَا إِسْمَاعِيلُ بْنُ جَعْفَرٍ، عَنْ عَبْدِ اللَّهِ بْنِ دِينَارٍ، عَنِ ابْنِ عُمَرَ، قَالَ قَالَ رَسُولُ اللَّهِ صلى الله عليه وسلم " إِنَّ مِنَ الشَّجَرِ شَجَرَةً لاَ يَسْقُطُ وَرَقُهَا، وَإِنَّهَا مَثَلُ الْمُسْلِمِ، فَحَدِّثُونِي مَا هِيَ ". فَوَقَعَ النَّاسُ فِي شَجَرِ الْبَوَادِي. قَالَ عَبْدُ اللَّهِ وَوَقَعَ فِي نَفْسِي أَنَّهَا النَّخْلَةُ، فَاسْتَحْيَيْتُ ثُمَّ قَالُوا حَدِّثْنَا مَا هِيَ يَا رَسُولَ اللَّهِ قَالَ " هِيَ النَّخْلَةُ ".

Allah's Messenger (ﷺ) said, "Amongst the trees, there is a tree, the leaves of which do not fall and is like a Muslim. Tell me the name of that tree." Everybody (companions of the prophet) started thinking about the trees of the desert areas. And I (Ibn Umar (ra) thought of the date-palm tree but felt shy to answer the others then asked, "What is that tree, O Allah's Messenger (ﷺ)?" He replied, "It is the date-palm tree. "Ibn Umar (ra) said he was the youngest from among them so he did speak...But when he told his father (Umar ibn al-Khattab (ra)), his father said, "if you had said so (gave the answer) that would have been more valuable to me than a reddish camel {something of value to the dessert Arabs}
[Sahih Bukhari book 3 number 58]

Instilling & building upon those characteristics helps to build a resistance to ambiguity that is prevalent in today's society. Secularization of the world from truth (*Religion is the source of all truth*) has caused a tail spin downward for humanity in the arena of his moral compass where religion is adopted into life only where it fits while everything else is discarded. Unfortunately, what many people discard is the most important, where the holidays & ritual practices are something that is common to most practitioners whether they do it or don't. But in essence the truth & adherence to the core of divine guidance and laws is lost...As things have become further and further distorted the unfamiliarity of situations and or information has caused many people to adopt the behavior of others. It's the actions of others as we observe that lead us into behaving often times in decadence towards our innate or pre-existing systems of belief, thinking & behavior. Feeling awkward, uncomfortable or uneasy are the signs we receive internally to adjust ourselves accordingly, but when the perception of our realities are altered by massive alterations in society with ambiguity then over time, with persistence, the subtle signs we get to something being wrong seize due to desensitized consciousness. Lack of knowledge causes following and therefore one follows group norms in the society they are. Other human weakness of wanting to fit in or be liked also lead to confirmative motives especially when someone may be viewed as the out-sider. Different cultures have different mental pictures and understanding or what is normal and what isn't. Many people today would argue in agreeance to democracy and "do as thou pleaseth" type of slogans of being...but on the contrary these concepts are fairly new coinciding with the west rise to power and with that their sphere of influence exported around the world to create that following of their concept of culture. With this rise to power came with it the ideals of superiority, narcissism, Machivivellian-ism, Darwin-ism and fascism...All of these Ism's have been undoing society instead of making it more just. In my opinion conformity is coupled unescapably to democracy and or "Mob Rule." Once the philosophical rhetoric is in place and the people aren't quite clever enough anymore in recognition to the changes being implemented, conformity with continue to morph into different shapes until the people are utterly ruined. Modernity is the contemporary way of giving things in the past a face-lift, but modernity has nothing to do with values/morals. The world could still undergo all the innovative changes that have made life easier while still holding to those principals. Wearing clothes vs fashionably naked, to having distinguishing manners and modesty doesn't interfere with modernity...However the lack thereof is detrimental to the fabric of society...

*As the ongoing debate over what exactly the Establishment Clause in the First Amendment of the United States Constitution means continues into the twenty-first century, the Supreme Court finds itself without a bright line rule proscribing where exactly America stands on the issue of "to what degree should America separate religion from state." Originating back to 1791 when the United States Constitution was officially ratified, the drafters granted **freedom of and from religion to those who wished to be part of America**. However, as time passed this freedom of and from religion began to take on new interpretations that the original drafters of the Constitution may not have foreseen.*

__Taken literally, the Establishment Clause does not mention anything about a "separation between church and state.__" This notion, which came about through a letter written by President Jefferson to the Danbury Connecticut Baptist Association in an effort to support the Establishment Clause, has now become a major source of discussion in the Supreme Court. __In fact, the Establishment Clause and this fiction of a "separation between church and state" have been the driving force in many Supreme Court decisions that have little to do with establishing a national religion.__ It seems as if they arise as a way for state institutions to stay politically correct, so to not offend the melting pot of American religions. (Hershorin, 2003).

On the other side of the scale, we always find the Islamic perspective mired in hate largely from **misunderstanding, disbelief** and Saudi Arabia's seemingly hastiness in carrying out punishment from reporting media sources. What is always overlooked are the conditions and the hearings that have to be undergone that conclude with capital punishments. Let's face it, what one sees & understands by living in a region is much different than the bias it acquires in order to persuade the masses of people. I'm not here to condemn nor condone the Arabian government, because although they have an Islamic government there are still problems that exist in it. However, the application of Islamic law (*shari'ah, which is divine law same that is in the Torah & Gospel with abrogation's in succession*), you will find that the deterrent is far greater in curbing undesired behavior than the actual punishment when it is applied justly. Many westerners who have moved to the middle-east have given testimony to the security & safety of their new environments...

When anyone of us observes the actions of others does the question ever arise within yourself as to rational behind the behavior you see from others? Sure, myself included, witness almost daily something of irrational behavior. So where is the law in this matter? Shouldn't the law itself be a deterrent to misbehavior of any kind? Behavior is often a hint to further actions but man's law allows crimes to occur and then seeks to sort them out with valid punishments afterward. We can never undo the victimization of a victim, so the effort should be for the former condition & not the latter. In fact, Hollywood adopted the concept in a Tom Cruise film called "Minority Report." In the film there is a pre-crime division that uses 3 oracle type beings to predict the future in eradicating crime in Washington D.C.; These oracles (still paired with pagan belief) is the distorted divine element in the movie; however in reality the Quran on the other hand continues to unfold in its gems of wisdoms as it is the source of ultimate truth. Of the primary conditions to witnessing for one's self as I mentioned toward acceptance of divine law is the subtle inclination that has led man to disbelief, and I say so because even those of Jewish, Christian & portions of Muslims in faith don't follow the laws within those previous & present revelation(s), which is usually of the portion I mentioned that is disregarded. All sorts of violations of 1st of the Ten Commandments, same sex marriage, eating of pork, pre-marital sex etc. are all violated in ignorance of divine law made permissive through conformity and legalization of societal authority & popular demand.

Magic

In addition, the severity of magic in all of its forms {horoscopes, fortune-tellers, Astron0my, amulets for protection, spells for love & evil, superstitions such as rabbits feet or knocking on wood...All but mislead attributing attributes that are only present with the Almighty Allah/God. These acts as well as seeking their aide are all forbidden & discern capital punishment because of their strong inclinations of misguidance}.

For example:

- Leviticus 20:27 ESV / "A man or a woman who is a medium or a necromancer shall surely be put to death. They shall be stoned with stones; their blood shall be upon them."

- Leviticus 19:31 ESV / "Do not turn to mediums or necromancers {in matters of prediction of the unseen world, magic, and fortune}; do not seek them out, and so make yourselves unclean by them: I am the Lord your God.

The bible even makes mention to some of the crimes against humanity and their resistance to divine governance, it points to the pending punishment...

- Revelation 21:8 ESV / But as for the cowardly, the faithless, the detestable, as for murderers, the sexually immoral, sorcerers, idolaters, and all liars, their portion will be in the lake that burns with fire and sulfur, which is the second death."

Finally, as a result to the denial of the people toward the creator; it also points to the conditions of the world today in its lawlessness and ambiguity of truth and love of falsehood.

- 2 Thessalonians 2:9 ESV / *The coming of the lawless one* is by the activity of Satan with all power and false signs and wonders,

The lawless one regarded in the above biblical verse is making mention to the Fitnah (*test/trials*) of 'Dajjal' {*the false Messiah/anti-Christ*}, which was spoken about by all Prophets of Allah/God...By design he will be given miracles by Allah to test mankind, and of these varying aspects of his testing humanity are the many attention gatherings of mediums, fortune-tellers, alien theories etc. These are all highly rooted in evil & dark magic of Jewish kabbalah, and contact with the Jinn who contract men/women into huge sacrilege contracts of selling themselves in return for worldly gain of fame, fortune & power.

Following hadith of Tamim Ad-Dari {*a Christian who accepted Islam in the time of Prophet Muhammad s.a.w.*} tells of a journey he and other companions of the prophet s.a.w. were on...he and the others later return to the prophet s.a.w and tell him of their great ordeal narrated from authentic narration below of 'Dajjal' and his release in the time of Muhammad s.a.w.

Fatimah bint Qais (RA) narrated that Allah's Prophet (PBUH) ascended the Minbar, he laughed and said, "Verily, Tamim Ad-Dari (a Christian who had embraced Islam) narrated a story to me, and it made me happy (*which agrees with what I was telling you about 'Al-Masih Ad-Dajjal'... as reported by Imam Muslim*), so I wanted to narrate it to you. Some people among the inhabitants of Palestine travelled by boat in the sea, taking them here and there (because of a storm), until it cast them on an island among the islands at sea (one month's journey from the holy land). There they found a beast, clothed with its hair, flowing out which made it hard to discern the head from its tale. They said: What are you? It said: I am 'Al-Jassasah'(meaning spy). They said: Give us some news. It said: I shall not give you any news, nor do I want any of your news. But go to the furthest village, for there is someone who will give you news and seek your news. So we (they) went to the furthest village, and there was a man fettered with chains. He said: Inform me about the spring of Zughar. We said: It is full and flowing. He said: Inform me about Al-Buhairah (i.e. Tiberias). We said: It is full & flowing. He said: Inform me about groves of Baysan which is between Jordan & Palestine, do they produce food? We said: Yes. He said: Inform me about the Prophet, who has he been sent? We said,"Yes." He said, "Inform me do the people follow him?" We said, "Yes." He replied, "it is best that they follow him; As for me I'm am Dajjal and have awaited my prescribe time.... "

(Hadith No. 2253, Chapters on Al-Fitan, Jami' At-Tirmidhi, Vol. 4; Hadith No. 7386 (2942), Book of Tribulations & Portents of the Hour, Sahih Muslim, Vol. 7).

So, 'Dajjal' is already released and is busy playing his tricks with us. He is among us and is spreading the Fitnah all around.

- A question arises: If he is already around, why can't we see him? The answer is simple (though people with limited or no knowledge of space and time will find it difficult to accept): 'Dajjal' is already among us, but he is in a different space and time coordinates. For example: Jinns and Angels are creations of Allah, and they exist along with us in this world. But, we cannot see them. Similarly, why can't 'Dajjal' be around among us without us being able to see him (as a person) by our naked eyes? So, **in order to see 'Dajjal' around and among us in present times, we have to use the eyes of our heart; and the eyes of the hearts can only see him if our hearts are enlightened by 'Noor' of Allah by faith and belief.**.if we look to the world and how its slowly turned inward out, where truth has become falsehood; while falsehood as become truth, divine laws that have been abrogated by man, even the disturbed harmony of the earth a she convulses from the corruption man has made on land & sea then we are able to see this lawless one within his current spiritual plane.

  However, there will be a time when 'Dajjal' will appear in form of a human being: **It was narrated that Umair bin Hani Al-Ansi said, "I heard Abdullah bin Umar (RA) saying: We were sitting with Allah's Messenger (PBUH) and he mentioned tribulations……. A man will rise as a believer in the morning, and come upon the evening as a disbeliever, until the people are split into two camps: the camp of Faith in which there will be no hypocrisy, and the camp of hypocrisy in which there will be no Faith. When that happens, (then) expects the 'Dajjal' on that day or the next."** (Hadith No. 4242, Book of Tribulations & Great Battles, Sunan Abu Dawud, Vol. 4).

So when the day comes that we see Medina (city in Eastern *Saudi Arabia whose ancient & biblical name is Yathrib*) it ruins of historical sites etc. then then day is near as the hadith explains: **It was narrated that Mua'dh bin Jabal (RA) said: Allah's Messenger (PBUH) said, "Jerusalem will flourish when Yathrib (i.e. Madinah) is in ruins, and Yathrib will be in ruins when the Great War occurs {WW3}. The Great War will occur when Constantinople is conquered, and Constantinople will be conquered when 'Dajjal' appears…"** (Hadith No. 4294, Book of Tribulations & Great Battles, Sunan Abu Dawud, Vol. 4).

We now find ourselves on the cusp of a great transition and as long as the world remains secular, infighting will ensue until one is overcome forcibly by the other, which is prophesied to be the religion of truth...Islam. Secularism is stooped in disbelief and ignores the responsibility of our divine purpose. I guess this is another premise to evolutionist in trying to coheres the belief of spontaneous life, therefore denying the authority that presides over us by our creator to being obedient, just, and mindful of our return to him. وَوَصَّيْنَا الْإِنسَانَ بِوَالِدَيْهِ حَمَلَتْهُ أُمُّهُ وَهْنًا عَلَىٰ وَهْنٍ وَفِصَالُهُ فِي عَامَيْنِ أَنِ اشْكُرْ لِي وَلِوَالِدَيْكَ إِلَيَّ الْمَصِيرُ

And We have enjoined upon man [care] for his parents. His mother carried him, [increasing her] in weakness upon weakness, and his weaning is in two years. Be grateful to Me and to your parents; to Me is the [final] destination [Luqman 31:14] وَإِن جَاهَدَاكَ عَلَىٰ أَن تُشْرِكَ بِي مَا لَيْسَ لَكَ بِهِ عِلْمٌ فَلَا تُطِعْهُمَا ۖ وَصَاحِبْهُمَا فِي الدُّنْيَا مَعْرُوفًا ۖ وَاتَّبِعْ سَبِيلَ مَنْ أَنَابَ إِلَيَّ ۚ ثُمَّ إِلَيَّ مَرْجِعُكُمْ

فَأُنَبِّئُكُم بِمَا كُنتُمْ تَعْمَلُونَ

But if they endeavor to make you associate with Me that of which you have no knowledge, do not obey them but accompany them in [this] world with appropriate kindness and follow the way of those who turn back to Me [in repentance]. Then to Me will be your return, and I will inform you about what you used to do. [Luqman 31:15]

The importance of truth is something of worthy attainment because without it the world is being stirred into despotism. It is as the Zimbardo Stanford Prison psychological test concluded. The test was administered to volunteers who were divided into prisoners and guards. The guards were then told to treat the prisoners in unjust ways of shock treatment with increasing levels of applied voltage to test their obedience to authority despite their own conscious toward these actions. What the test found was that most remained obedient until the end. This experiment followed WWII, in better trying to understand how people can follow wrong authority against belief. Zimbardo stated: *"When ordinary people are put into novel, evil place such as most prisons the "situation always wins" & people lose."*

Influence Agents

In Islam, there is nothing wrong with conformity as long as conformity doesn't derail or supersede the commands of the almighty. Islam recognizes the potential of humanity and forecast his initiatives in all aspects of life, and thus provides a comprehensive way of sustaining, preserving and legislating all life. This functionality itself its proof of its divine source as no other text is able to answer all of humanities sufferings, but again the acceptance boils down to belief. The Secular world is working to encourage humanity to abandon religious belief by grouping it all into controlling apparatuses to be applied over mankind; and that is true in regards to "man's version" which he has altered and manipulated. For example: the very premise behind Jesus (as) dying on the cross for the sins of humanity is not to embed deep gratitude with furtherance of oneself from committing sin; instead it's to enable & encourage people to freely do as they wish. Claiming with one's mouth **only** (*not with daily living in deeds that marry word with deed*), millions claim to be saved and granted the abode of paradise all after living a life of careless, selfish sin...It makes no since. Not even in this current world are people excused for crimes they commit so why is it that people would attribute this lowly action to Allah/God? As more people are enlightened to the absurdity of these dogmatic alterations thanks in part to negative media of Islam that has invoked many into their own understanding of the demonization of Islam. They ultimately find what is desperately fought against to further conceal the masses from understanding. The reality is Islam can't be altered because its preserved in the original text of Arabic and authentic narrations of the prophet s.a.w. due to Allah's promise and all of the scholarly work that followed the generations of the prophet's companions (ra). This has left only the fraudulent acting out of participants & apostates with plenty of media coverage and funding of covert proxies war's that allow the true faces & political motives of those actors to remain hidden.

أَفَغَيْرَ اللهِ أَبْتَغِي حَكَمًا وَهُوَ الَّذِي أَنزَل إِلَيْكُمُ الْكِتَابَ مُفَصَّلاً ۚ وَالَّذِينَ آتَيْنَاهُمُ الْكِتَابَ يَعْلَمُونَ أَنَّهُ مُنَزَّلٌ مِّن رَّبِّكَ بِالْحَقِّ ۖ فَلا تَكُونَنَّ مِنَ الْمُمْتَرِينَ

[Say], "Then is it other than Allah I should seek as judge while it is He who has revealed to you the Book explained in detail?" And those to whom We [previously] gave the Scripture know that it is sent down from your Lord in truth, so never be among the doubters. [Al-An'am 6:114]

وَتَمَّتْ كَلِمَتُ رَبِّكَ صِدْقًا وَعَدْلاً ۚ لاَّ مُبَدِّلَ لِكَلِمَاتِهِ ۚ وَهُوَ السَّمِيعُ الْعَلِيمُ

And the word of your Lord has been fulfilled in truth and in justice. None can alter His words, and He is the Hearing, the Knowing [Al-An'am 6:115]

وَإِن تُطِعْ أَكْثَرَ مَن فِي الْأَرْضِ يُضِلُّوكَ عَن سَبِيلِ اللهِ ۚ إِن يَتَّبِعُونَ إِلَّا الظَّنَّ وَإِنْ هُمْ إِلَّا يَخْرُصُونَ

And if you obey most of those upon the earth, they will mislead you from the way of Allah. They follow not except assumption, and they are not but falsifying. [Al-An'am 6:116] إِنَّ رَبَّكَ هُوَ أَعْلَمُ مَن يَضِلُّ عَن سَبِيلِهِ وَهُوَ أَعْلَمُ بِالْمُهْتَدِينَ

indeed, your Lord is most knowing of who strays from His way, and He is most knowing of the [rightly] guided. [Al-An'am 6:117]

Propagandist, press agents or publicity men employing tactics in the same manner that persuades our consumption & spending habits; often with subliminal undertones that is far more powerful than that at the conscious level. In our own complexity (human design) it's literally our own ignorance's about ourselves that are played against us making life unharmonious with our own nature and the whole of creation in general.

Social-psychologist Robert Cialdini suggests 6 simple principles as to how people are persuaded & thereby conform #2 & #3 are combined...

1. **Reciprocity**: Reciprocity is the natural balance of duality, give and take of society; but in terms of obligation he suggests people are trained from childhood to abide by rule or suffer social disapproval. In addition future obligations anticipate future continuing relationships, transactions & exchanges in society.

   How It's Exploited

   Rule can apply to uninvited exchanges -- when exploited, others can reduce our ability to freely decide, and thus, lead us to react automatically

Since society is guided by its rule, if it itself isn't held to a disciplinary hierarchy that supersedes its power then corruption will surely come about with human inclinations of bad behavior. We all know that life comes with obligations in order to sustain it; however spirituality should be first preceding life itself, along with the realization & importance to one-accordance collectivism over individualism, because unless there is accordance to higher purpose humanities cohesiveness will deteriorate, differ, and split into opposing fractions making life more difficult than it should be.

وَلَقَدْ صَرَّفْنَا فِي هَذَا الْقُرْآنِ لِلنَّاسِ مِن كُلِّ مَثَلٍ ۚ وَكَانَ الْإِنسَانُ أَكْثَرَ شَيْءٍ جَدَلًا

And We have certainly diversified in this Qur'an for the people from every [kind of] example; but man has ever been, most of anything, [prone to] dispute. [Al-Kahf 18:54]

2. Commitment and Consistency:

- **Social Proof** A means to determine what is correct by finding out what other people think is correct usually through observation test of behavior as a measure of what is acceptable over changing time periods. Acceptable in the degree we see others performing it. Other tools are thus employed in helping to change these principles especially today. Creators of habit (human-beings) we are easily stimulated into compliance by informing the individual that many other individuals have been complying (unanimous compliance and compliance by famous or authoritative people is most effective).

Since we are habitual in most of what we do, it is second nature for many to follow the pact. This compulsion to do as others are doing because they are superior in number is in many cases enough visual proof for many. This is a false attribution of truth to be in connection to those who are the majority as you will often find that it is merely desire at the base of these motives.

أَفَرَأَيْتَ مَنِ اتَّخَذَ إِلَهَهُ هَوَاهُ وَأَضَلَّهُ اللَّهُ عَلَى عِلْمٍ وَخَتَمَ عَلَى سَمْعِهِ وَقَلْبِهِ وَجَعَلَ عَلَى بَصَرِهِ غِشَاوَةً فَمَن يَهْدِيهِ مِن بَعْدِ اللَّهِ ۚ أَفَلَا تَذَكَّرُونَ

Have you seen he who has taken as his god his [own] desire, and Allah has sent him astray due to knowledge and has set a seal upon his hearing and his heart and put over his vision a veil? So who will guide him after Allah? Then will you not be reminded? [Al-Jathiya 45:23]

وَقَالُوا مَا هِيَ إِلَّا حَيَاتُنَا الدُّنْيَا نَمُوتُ وَنَحْيَا وَمَا يُهْلِكُنَا إِلَّا الدَّهْرُ ۚ وَمَا لَهُم بِذَٰلِكَ مِنْ عِلْمٍ ۖ إِنْ هُمْ إِلَّا يَظُنُّونَ

And they say, "There is not but our worldly life; we die and live, and nothing destroys us except time." And they have of that no knowledge; they are only assuming. [Al-Jathiya 45:24]

وَإِن تُطِعْ أَكْثَرَ مَن فِي الْأَرْضِ يُضِلُّوكَ عَن سَبِيلِ اللَّهِ ۚ إِن يَتَّبِعُونَ إِلَّا الظَّنَّ وَإِنْ هُمْ إِلَّا يَخْرُصُونَ As a result

And if you obey most of those upon the earth, they will mislead you from the way of Allah. They follow not except assumption, and they are not but falsifying. [Al-An'am 6:116]

3. **Liking** People prefer to say "yes" to individuals they know and like

We place a lot of influence on appearance and what it appeasing to the eye therefore it is by these same tangible factors that we are hooked into cohersion. Experts have long realized the human compulsion toward what looks good and to what appeals to their likeability.

- o Physical attractiveness often does far more than just gain our attention; it envelops the whole with a sort of "halo-affect" that is applied to the entire thing. The better something looks, the more flawless it is, and more perfect, correct and successful it will be. This is a perceptionary flaw within man that has become the commodity of selling tactics from products, services, and even our leadership.
- o Similarity is instinctual, as we all have a natural gravitational pull toward things, places, and people we are more familiar & similar too. In opposition dis-similarity can be exploited in order to persuade incorrectness, evils, & hatred...
- o Praise; the more something is praised the attention is paid toward it...Celebrity is a perfect example as they often rotate in their time of media attention in building their public image. When this praise begins to dwindle, you see them always jockeying for prominent roles of hits in order to recharge that praise. Praise can be addictive to the ego, so it can also be used to corrupt individuals through egocentricity means...
- o Association; is a means by which also is suitable to our egos in making us feel more connected. This connectedness provides an enabling satisfaction that gives us more credit than what our own natural abilities offer.
- o Shadowing; for many people becomes a means by which they build their outward appearance and or personalities mimicking traits of character of those they view in ways that can attribute the same to themselves.

Cialdini's suggestion to combating these principals actually falls in line with Islamic principles; his advice is for the person(s) to be critical of the concepts and or bias that might be lining these actions with deception. Furthermore he suggests viewing the request alone outside of the opinions or image of the requestor. This might allow one to see things more clearly, and remove emotional influences from the drive towards acceptance.

The Quran says:

إِنَّمَا أَمْوَالُكُمْ وَأَوْلَادُكُمْ فِتْنَةٌ ۚ وَاللَّهُ عِندَهُ أَجْرٌ عَظِيمٌ

> Your wealth and your children are but a trial, and Allah has with Him a great reward. [At-Taghabun 64:15]

زُيِّنَ للنَّاسِ حُبُّ الشَّهَوَاتِ مِنَ النِّسَاءِ وَالْبَنِينَ وَالْقَنَاطِيرِ الْمُقَنطَرَةِ مِنَ الذَّهَبِ وَالْفِضَّةِ وَالْخَيْلِ الْمُسَوَّمَةِ وَالْأَنْعَامِ وَالْحَرْثِ ۗ ذَٰلِكَ مَتَاعُ الْحَيَاةِ الدُّنْيَا ۖ وَاللَّهُ عِندَهُ حُسْنُ الْمَآبِ

> Beautified for people is the love of that which they desire - of women and sons, heaped-up sums of gold and silver, fine branded horses, and cattle and tilled land. That is the enjoyment of worldly life, but Allah has with Him the best return. [Al-Imran 3:14]

Both of these Quranic verses could be discussed in great detail, because although reading it one can derive the fundamental meaning, it often has much more wisdom therein. For example: the latter verse mentions the desire of people and it lists them. Pay close attention to how Allah mentions them...He says women, sons (represent family strength), wealth, fine branded horses (would amount to fine automobiles today), cattle & tilled land (would imply business). He lists these desires this way because this is the order in which it upon man. Influences thereby that pair the success of obtaining this life's pleasures are sold with glitz & glamour; but as the first verse mentions: "Our spouses and children are but a trial for us." Problems within the family are prevalent within society today, as the cohesion of the family unit has been attacked. Two-parent working families, neglect of the children, and chasing materialism has all subjugated the collectivism of the family and made it nuclear; radioactive in closeness so each is compelled in their own ways to worldly goals...

4. **Authority** is portrayed in the company of high levels of knowledge, wisdom, and power...hence the importance of outward appearance, stature, body-language, verbal eloquence, and the projection of strength all helping individual(s) obtain & sustain the projection of authority. Authority is something today that has transitioned from entitlement of true possession of the above qualities to those in possession of wealth. Amassed Wealth has replaced the rule of authority with justice to the lawless, abasement of desire. Many experiments have been conducted all seeking to understand further this notion as to how authority can be most effectively applied. In earlier times authority was paired with physical strength, Evil, Magic, and divinity...All were a means of justification and succession to rule. The mental state of the population is thus very important to the critical application of authority, so people need not be so independent or free thinking as to under mind the authority in place. So Importance is given to:
   o Titles
   o Clothing (expensive suits, uniforms, symbols of authority)
   o Authoritative Locations (inaccessibility, security appearance etc.)
   o Automobiles (association with wealth, privilege, power)

These are all the necessary projections to give legitimacy to their authority but it is all the illusion they put forward. Be sensitive to changes in authorities' behavior, demands over time, from initially acceptable to ultimately abusive and unjust. There are a number of hadith that embody this principle of change narrated by bulk of sahabiat (ra) (companions to the prophet s.a.w) one such narration reads:

Volume 9, Book 88, Number 174:

Narrated Sahl bin Sa'd:

*I heard the Prophet saying, "I am your predecessor at the Lake-Fount (Kauthar){**beyond the day of Judgement in spiritual world**} , and whoever will come to it, will drink from it, and whoever will drink from it, will never become thirsty after that. There will come to me some people whom I know and they know me, and then a barrier will be set up between me and them." Abu Sa'id Al-Khudri added that the Prophet further said: "I will say, "Those people are from me." It will be said, 'You do not know what changes and new things they did after you.' Then I will say, 'Far removed (from mercy), far removed (from mercy), those who changed (the religion) after me! "*

These changes and new things people do are the innovations that they have adapted in exploiting power. Authority is meant to be just and consistent throughout time never differing, but innovation(s) are something that need constant modification because man is not sufficient enough to administer every aspect of life present & future tense that will be justly, and accurately protected under the initiation of that law. Although abrogation has come from Allah/God with succession of revelation concluding with the Quran, it is not his deficiency but it is his mercy and encompassing knowledge of all things to guide us from successive generations in our evolution or decadence. In addition, he the most high knew that previous generations would corrupt and altogether destroy previous scripture and this was also a reason for his succeeding books.

Figure 2 United Nations spider Web Logo

The Quran says:

مَثَلُ الَّذِينَ اتَّخَذُوا مِن دُونِ اللهِ أَوْلِيَاءَ كَمَثَلِ الْعَنكَبُوتِ اتَّخَذَتْ بَيْتًا ۖ وَإِنَّ أَوْهَنَ الْبُيُوتِ لَبَيْتُ الْعَنكَبُوتِ ۖ لَوْ كَانُوا يَعْلَمُونَ

The example of **those who take allies other than Allah** {*Allah's sovereignty is overlooked and man's law and authority are placed above him*} is like that of the spider who takes a home. And indeed, the weakest of homes is the home of the spider, if they only knew. [Al-Ankabut 29:41].

This verse brings to the surface of our understanding the evil that lies within man and his cloaked agenda and true purpose of the U.N. whose logo employs the spider's Web in its logo; indicating its control over the world...

5. **Scarcity**

People assign more value to opportunities when they are less available—if there are fewer resources and less time to get them, we want it more. In my opinion this is the whole premise behind tiered classification. This concept helps to fuel demand and thus by that influence has momentum to conform.

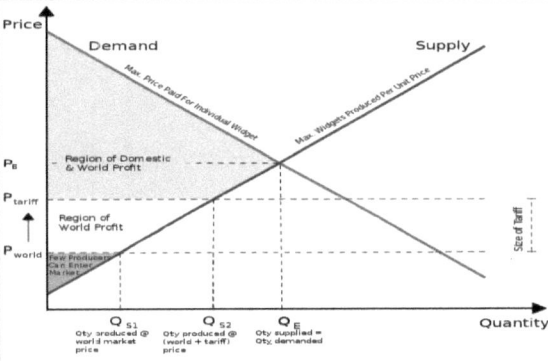

Figure 3 supply and demand

No different from the concepts that control market(s) value, so does scarcity do a similar alternative upon the psyche of humanity. Poverty has always been a tactic used within the strategies of war that help to drive home the new ideals to be applied.

- Use of this principle for profit can be seen in compliance techniques as a 'limited number' and or 'deadline' tactics in which persuaders try to convince us that access is restricted by amount or by time.

Bush administration used a variation of this theme in justifying rush to war in Iraq: time is running out for Saddam unless we stop him now he will use his WMD against us (Zimbardo, 2006). Here in lies the dangers of wrong values applied to scarcity which is be manipulated only to direct a desired outcome. Attribution error happens when we underestimate a situation and overestimate the person's disposition…Even in light of evidence that was reported back by inspectors from the U.N. the administration chose to ignore it, and promoted their want instead piggy-backing American sentiment & emotion that allowed a host of political & legislative adaptations as a result.

The Quran says in reference to combating the image of scarcity:
Today materialism is promoted in translation of doctrine in order to further the campaign of fascism as people become more so allured by affluent lifestyles. Wealth is

NOT an indication of blessing as lack is not an indication of punishment...both have elements of reward and consequence respectively, but in & of themselves as they are readily applied today is false. Allah/God says

أَحَسِبَ النَّاسُ أَن يُتْرَكُوا أَن يَقُولُوا آمَنَّا وَهُمْ لَا يُفْتَنُونَ:

Do the people think that they will be left to say, "We believe" and they will not be tried? [Al-Ankabut 29:2]

وَلَقَدْ فَتَنَّا الَّذِينَ مِن قَبْلِهِمْ فَلَيَعْلَمَنَّ اللَّهُ الَّذِينَ صَدَقُوا وَلَيَعْلَمَنَّ الْكَاذِبِينَ

But We have certainly tried those before them, and Allah will surely make evident those who are truthful, and He will surely make evident the liars.[Al-Ankabut 29:3]

Every condition therefore should be regarded within divine plan and premise; held with patience & justice towards yourself and others that may have been placed in your charge. Scarcity in the world today is due to mans' greed and the policies that are implemented that exploited against ethnic groups and countries in efforts to manipulated the value(s) of natural resources, currency, & labor. Those who mislead by false authority

وَقَالَ الَّذِينَ كَفَرُوا لِلَّذِينَ آمَنُوا اتَّبِعُوا سَبِيلَنَا وَلْنَحْمِلْ خَطَايَاكُمْ وَمَا هُم بِحَامِلِينَ مِنْ خَطَايَاهُم مِّن شَيْءٍ إِنَّهُمْ لَكَاذِبُونَ

And those who disbelieve say to those who believe, "Follow our way, and we will carry your sins." But they will not carry anything of their sins. Indeed, they are liars. [Al-Ankabut 29:12]

وَلَيَحْمِلُنَّ أَثْقَالَهُمْ وَأَثْقَالًا مَّعَ أَثْقَالِهِمْ وَلَيُسْأَلُنَّ يَوْمَ الْقِيَامَةِ عَمَّا كَانُوا يَفْتَرُونَ

But they will surely carry their [own] burdens and [others they helped provoke others to do] burdens along with their burdens, and they will surely be questioned on the Day of Resurrection about what they used to invent. [Al-Ankabut 29:13]

Because of the psychological draw scarcity can have on man in all of our drives that can be used against us, Allah/God further commands us:

إِنَّ الْمُبَذِّرِينَ كَانُوا إِخْوَانَ الشَّيَاطِينِ وَكَانَ الشَّيْطَانُ لِرَبِّهِ كَفُورًا

Indeed, the wasteful are brothers of the devils, and ever has Satan been to his Lord ungrateful.

وَإِمَّا تُعْرِضَنَّ عَنْهُمُ ابْتِغَاءَ رَحْمَةٍ مِّن رَّبِّكَ تَرْجُوهَا فَقُل لَّهُمْ قَوْلًا مَّيْسُورًا

And if you [must] turn away from the needy {not having anything to give or offer them} awaiting mercy from your Lord which you expect, then speak to them a gentle word.

وَلَا تَجْعَلْ يَدَكَ مَغْلُولَةً إِلَىٰ عُنُقِكَ وَلَا تَبْسُطْهَا كُلَّ الْبَسْطِ فَتَقْعُدَ مَلُومًا مَّحْسُورًا

And do not make your hand [as] chained to your neck or extend it completely {never giving or giving too much to impoverish yourself} and [thereby] become blamed and insolvent.

إِنَّ رَبَّكَ يَبْسُطُ الرِّزْقَ لِمَن يَشَاءُ وَيَقْدِرُ ۚ إِنَّهُ كَانَ بِعِبَادِهِ خَبِيرًا بَصِيرًا

Indeed, your Lord extends provision for whom He wills and restricts [it]. Indeed He is ever, concerning His servants, Acquainted and Seeing.

وَلَا تَقْتُلُوا أَوْلَادَكُمْ خَشْيَةَ إِمْلَاقٍ ۖ نَّحْنُ نَرْزُقُهُمْ وَإِيَّاكُمْ ۚ إِنَّ قَتْلَهُمْ كَانَ خِطْئًا كَبِيرًا

And do not kill your children for fear of poverty {abortion}. We provide for them and for you. Indeed, their killing is ever a great sin.

وَلَا تَقْرَبُوا الزِّنَا ۖ إِنَّهُ كَانَ فَاحِشَةً وَسَاءَ سَبِيلًا

And do not approach unlawful sexual intercourse. Indeed, it is ever an immorality and is evil as a way.

وَلَا تَقْتُلُوا النَّفْسَ الَّتِي حَرَّمَ اللَّهُ إِلَّا بِالْحَقِّ ۗ وَمَن قُتِلَ مَظْلُومًا فَقَدْ جَعَلْنَا لِوَلِيِّهِ سُلْطَانًا فَلَا يُسْرِف فِّي الْقَتْلِ ۖ إِنَّهُ كَانَ مَنصُورًا

And do not kill the soul {ourselves or others} which Allah has forbidden, **except by right**. And whoever is killed unjustly - We have given his heir authority {life for a life, eye for an eye}, but let him not exceed limits in [the matter of] taking life. Indeed, he has been supported [by the law].

وَلَا تَقْرَبُوا مَالَ الْيَتِيمِ إِلَّا بِالَّتِي هِيَ أَحْسَنُ حَتَّىٰ يَبْلُغَ أَشُدَّهُ ۚ وَأَوْفُوا بِالْعَهْدِ ۖ إِنَّ الْعَهْدَ كَانَ مَسْئُولًا

And do not approach the property of an orphan {taking anything from their wealth while you are in care of them}, except in the way that is best {in helping to provide for them}, until he reaches maturity {when you can turn over their wealth to them}. And fulfill [every] commitment. Indeed, the commitment is ever [that about which one will be] questioned.

وَأَوْفُوا الْكَيْلَ إِذَا كِلْتُمْ وَزِنُوا بِالْقِسْطَاسِ الْمُسْتَقِيمِ ۚ ذَٰلِكَ خَيْرٌ وَأَحْسَنُ تَأْوِيلًا

And give full measure when you measure, and weigh with an even balance {business transactions} . That is the best [way] and best in result.

وَلَا تَقْفُ مَا لَيْسَ لَكَ بِهِ عِلْمٌ ۚ إِنَّ السَّمْعَ وَالْبَصَرَ وَالْفُؤَادَ كُلُّ أُولَٰئِكَ كَانَ عَنْهُ مَسْئُولًا

And do not pursue that of which you have no knowledge {spreading lies or untruth to promote cohersed responses}. Indeed, the hearing, the sight and the heart - about all those [one] will be questioned.

وَلَا تَمْشِ فِي الْأَرْضِ مَرَحًا ۖ إِنَّكَ لَن تَخْرِقَ الْأَرْضَ وَلَن تَبْلُغَ الْجِبَالَ طُولًا

And do not walk upon the earth exultantly. Indeed, you will never tear the earth [apart], and you will never reach the mountains in height {of arrogance and keeping these negative traits from being shadowed}.

كُلُّ ذَٰلِكَ كَانَ سَيِّئُهُ عِندَ رَبِّكَ مَكْرُوهًا

All that - its evil is ever, in the sight of your Lord, detested.

ذَٰلِكَ مِمَّا أَوْحَىٰ إِلَيْكَ رَبُّكَ مِنَ الْحِكْمَةِ ۗ وَلَا تَجْعَلْ مَعَ اللَّهِ إِلَٰهًا آخَرَ فَتُلْقَىٰ فِي جَهَنَّمَ مَلُومًا مَّدْحُورًا

That is from what your Lord has revealed to you, [O Muhammad], of wisdom. And, [O mankind], do not make [as equal] with Allah another deity, lest you be thrown into Hell, blamed and banished. [Al-Isra 17:27-39]

Placebic Reasons

Arguments that appear to make sense but are actually vacuous, lacking information or can even be detrimental to one's own health. For example, Edward Bernays, an Austrian-American pioneer in the field of public relations and propaganda, once induced the action of a women's liberation movement. Communicating with some debutants he was acquainted with and utilizing the power of the newspaper. The campaign was coined torches of freedom. Bernays hired these women to march in the Easter Sunday day Parade in 1929, while marching these women smoked cigarettes (their torches of freedom). The newspaper promoted it throughout the country and before long there was a significant increase of women smokers throughout the country...

Prior to this propaganda event, the habit of smoking was in the 17th century was promoted by Dutch painters as human foolishness, in the 19th century it adopted stereotypes linked to fallen women and prostitutes. Otherwise lost cases of women actually been jailed for smoking and or in the presence of their children [as in the case of Jennie Lasher who was sentenced to 30 days in jail. In 1908 the New York City Board of

Aldermen unanimously passed an ordinance that prohibited smoking by women in public. (Wikipedia)

What wasn't realized was the deliberate want of the tobacco companies to target and open up the market of smoking amongst women. Just one year prior in 1928 George Washington Hill, president of the American Tobacco Company said, "it will be like opening up a gold mine right in our front yard." Hill was the responsible person for hiring Bernays, who then later consulted with psycho-analysis Abraham Brill who was also of Austrian background arriving in America at the age of 15yrs.

What I often find interesting is always the trajectory of secular history prior to secularization. Almost always you will find present the adoption of divine law and laws that protected or prevented certain actions from being carried out in governance of earlier times with a systematic shift to its eradication. Furthermore the same complaints they offer against other people, you will find a double standard that goes against their own past actions. Human beings are just very quick at forgetting especially after adaptation; however this systematic declined was scripted in 1871 From the monologues of Albert Pike; **The First World War** was to be fought so as to enable the Illuminati to overthrow the powers of the Tsars in Russia and turn that country into the stronghold of Atheistic-Communism. The differences stirred up by agent {agents all hold key positions in government throughout the world} of the Illuminati between the British and German Empires were to be used to foment this war. After the war ended, Communism was to be built up and **used to destroy other governments and weaken religions**. **World War Two,** was to be fomented by using the differences between Fascists and Political Zionists. This war was to be fought so that Nazism would be destroyed and the **power of Political Zionism increased** so that the sovereign state of Israel could be established in Palestine. <u>**During World War Two International Communism was to be built up until it equalled in strength that of united Christendom**</u>. At this point it was to be contained and kept in check **<u>until</u>** required for the final social cataclysm. Can any informed person deny Roosevelt and Churchill did put this policy into effect? (Corrobated by Dr. Dennis L. Cuddy PhD). Following World War 2 the moral values and faith practices of Christianity have declined rapidly leaving a huge vacuum...Filling that void with the decline & uncovered truth of Christianity by many of its followers is Islam. Unfortunately, to a relinquished, significant amount and their successive generations who have grown up in a world lacking moral & spiritual responsibility the purity of Islam is connoted with extremist commentary; instead on the contrary it's really just calling people back to what they have abandoned. Nonetheless, In keeping with the scripted desired outcome...**World War Three** is to be fomented by using the differences the agent {of the Illuminati}stirrup between Political Zionists and the leaders of the Muslim world. The war is to be directed in such a manner that Islam (the Arab World) and Political Zionism (including the State of Israel) will destroy themselves while at the same time the remaining nations, once more divided against each other on this issue, will be forced to fight themselves into a state of complete exhaustion physically, mentally, spiritually and economically. Can any unbiased and reasoning person deny that the intrigue now going on in the Near, Middle, and Far East is designed to accomplish this devilish purpose? (Swift, 2015)

My reason for mentioning this is provoked by the actions in this highlighted case of the American Tobacco Company under the leadership of G.W. Hill. His deliberate campaign to target women in order to grow the market was something far more than just a market share conquest...Strategies such as this were literally victimizing the way of life of generations to come by this perceived twist in the consciousness of the people toward a renewed acceptance of a previously-detested practice. As successful as these under-minding campaigns were, they were all built on the premise of hollow arguments, while keeping pace with scripted direction of his-stories desired outcome. As a result we have noticed more policy written & controlled by Corporations as this allegory of rule operates from the shadows directing its operantants throughout every rung of society.

Pathologists in the 1930s just a year after these women's campaigns for smoking had started noticing the capacity of cigarette smoke to cause ciliastasis—the deadening of the tiny whip or hair-like structures lining the upper airway passages... structures known to be responsible for wafting particulate contaminants out of the lungs. Amongst the earliest documented research submitted for consideration was that from Claude Teague in his confidential 1953 'Survey of Cancer Research', written for upper management at RJ Reynolds, makers of Camel cigarettes, concluded that the parallel rise in cigarette use and cancer had led to the suspicion that tobacco was 'an important etiologic factor in the induction of primary cancer of the lung." (Proctor, 2011).

وَلَا تَقْتُلُوا النَّفْسَ الَّتِي حَرَّمَ اللَّهُ إِلَّا بِالْحَقِّ ۗ وَمَن قُتِلَ مَظْلُومًا فَقَدْ جَعَلْنَا لِوَلِيِّهِ سُلْطَانًا فَلَا يُسْرِف فِّي الْقَتْلِ ۖ إِنَّهُ كَانَ مَنصُورًا

And do not kill the soul {ourselves {smoking would fall under this same prohibition or others} which Allah has forbidden, **except by right** {*this implies self defense or capital punishment*}. And whoever is killed unjustly - We have given his heir authority {life for a life, eye for an eye}, but let him not exceed limits in [the matter of] taking life. Indeed, he has been supported [by the law]. [Al-Isra 17:33]

يَا أَيُّهَا الَّذِينَ آمَنُوا إِنَّمَا الْخَمْرُ وَالْمَيْسِرُ وَالْأَنصَابُ وَالْأَزْلَامُ رِجْسٌ مِّنْ عَمَلِ الشَّيْطَانِ فَاجْتَنِبُوهُ لَعَلَّكُمْ تُفْلِحُونَ

O you who have believed, indeed, intoxicants, gambling, [sacrificing on] stone alters [to other than Allah], and divining arrows are but defilement from the work of Satan, so avoid it that you may be successful.[Al-Maida 5:90]

إِنَّمَا يُرِيدُ الشَّيْطَانُ أَن يُوقِعَ بَيْنَكُمُ الْعَدَاوَةَ وَالْبَغْضَاءَ فِي الْخَمْرِ وَالْمَيْسِرِ وَيَصُدَّكُمْ عَن ذِكْرِ اللَّهِ وَعَنِ الصَّلَاةِ ۖ فَهَلْ أَنتُم مُّنتَهُونَ

Satan only wants to cause between you animosity and hatred through intoxicants and gambling and to avert you from the remembrance of Allah and from prayer. So will you not desist?[Al-Maida 5:91]

The Occult

As a result to propaganda our societies are morphing into extreme forms of individualism that only recognizes largely in part that which they have bought into. The world grossly mislead with a large portion weakened & indoctrinated in terms of religion, has shaped the collective aspects to ideologies, culture and or geography. This mutation has in fact been the central process of transformation of humanity to a more evil base as these propagandist and public relations experts exploit the population in brainwashing tactics in de-humanizing the human being. These fostered or tailor-made ways of thinking changes the perception of one against another in ways that defeat our abilities of seeing other human beings as human. This clouded judgment is born of repeated rhetoric and misleading information that is geared to grouping the mindset of people against the targeted group(s) in which the information is delivered. As a result we see that political alignment of groups based on wrong information, ideology, and geo-political power struggles...

Extreme times call for extreme measures, and the social influences used are aimed at ownership of those in whom they target. Providing a "total situation" in which their members live, interact, and work...Becoming the new family, substituting real family and friends with this academy of like affiliation.

Modifying the point of view of the group

This is the objective and the means by which people will concur. From the statesmen, to the journalist, to the preacher, and lecturers of all sorts not excluding academia are all employed in this very well organized network that is aimed at shifting public opinion. However, the list of measures is much longer since most types of manipulations begin fair earlier for free-thinking promoted societies such as Europe & United States which has helped to bring about its world power, but now the new phase of control over the world also requires the control of its internal populations...In analysis of the clients in comparison to the overall objective, this lays the foundation by which the manipulation will take shape. Employing different professions and having people from every rung of society help to give that perspective in input at further shaping those groups with the materials presented to them in manipulating their opinions. Again, Ambiguity finds a place of use among people who don't take it upon themselves to acquire real knowledge and or they allow themselves to be turned against the truth when it is presented to them out of arrogance, traditions, or societal status quo. In my opinion the largest manipulation to ever acquire in recent history is this manipulation of the Christian faith that deifies Eesa ibn Mariam a.s. (Jesus), which is the foundation of which this faith is built. Despite ALL the new out-spoken corrections and wrongful admittance of Christian scholars and the exit from the faith by thousands (which continues), still we find this deeply ingrained manipulation resistant in the world. In addition we find this alliance with certain Christian groups aligned with Israel...

يَا أَيُّهَا الَّذِينَ آمَنُوا لَا تَتَّخِذُوا الْيَهُودَ وَالنَّصَارَىٰ أَوْلِيَاءَ ۘ بَعْضُهُمْ أَوْلِيَاءُ بَعْضٍ ۚ وَمَن يَتَوَلَّهُم مِّنكُمْ فَإِنَّهُ مِنْهُمْ ۗ إِنَّ اللَّهَ لَا يَهْدِي الْقَوْمَ الظَّالِمِينَ

O you who have believed, do not take the Jews and the Christians as allies. They are [in fact] allies of one another. And whoever is an ally to them among you - then indeed, he is [one] of them. Indeed, Allah guides not the wrongdoing people. [Al-Maida 5:51]

فَتَرَى الَّذِينَ فِي قُلُوبِهِم مَّرَضٌ يُسَارِعُونَ فِيهِمْ يَقُولُونَ نَخْشَىٰ أَن تُصِيبَنَا دَائِرَةٌ ۚ فَعَسَى اللَّهُ أَن يَأْتِيَ بِالْفَتْحِ أَوْ أَمْرٍ مِّنْ عِندِهِ فَيُصْبِحُوا عَلَىٰ مَا أَسَرُّوا فِي أَنفُسِهِمْ نَادِمِينَ

So you see those in whose hearts is disease hastening into [association with] them, saying, "We are afraid a misfortune may strike us." But perhaps Allah will bring conquest or a decision from Him, and they will become, over what they have been concealing within themselves, regretful. [Al-Maida 5-52]

وَيَقُولُ الَّذِينَ آمَنُوا أَهَٰؤُلَاءِ الَّذِينَ أَقْسَمُوا بِاللَّهِ جَهْدَ أَيْمَانِهِمْ ۙ إِنَّهُمْ لَمَعَكُمْ ۚ حَبِطَتْ أَعْمَالُهُمْ فَأَصْبَحُوا خَاسِرِينَ

And those who believe will say, "Are these the ones who swore by Allah their strongest oaths that indeed they were with you?" Their deeds have become worthless, and they have become losers.[Al-Maida 5-53]

يَا أَيُّهَا الَّذِينَ آمَنُوا مَن يَرْتَدَّ مِنكُمْ عَن دِينِهِ فَسَوْفَ يَأْتِي اللَّهُ بِقَوْمٍ يُحِبُّهُمْ وَيُحِبُّونَهُ أَذِلَّةٍ عَلَى الْمُؤْمِنِينَ أَعِزَّةٍ عَلَى الْكَافِرِينَ يُجَاهِدُونَ فِي سَبِيلِ اللَّهِ وَلَا يَخَافُونَ لَوْمَةَ لَائِمٍ ۚ ذَٰلِكَ فَضْلُ اللَّهِ يُؤْتِيهِ مَن يَشَاءُ ۚ وَاللَّهُ وَاسِعٌ عَلِيمٌ

O you who have believed, whoever of you should revert from his religion - Allah will bring forth [in place of them] a people He will love and who will love Him [who are] humble toward the believers, powerful against the disbelievers; they strive in the cause of Allah and do not fear the blame of a critic. That is the favor of Allah; He bestows it upon whom He wills. And Allah is all-Encompassing and Knowing.[Al-Maida 5-54]

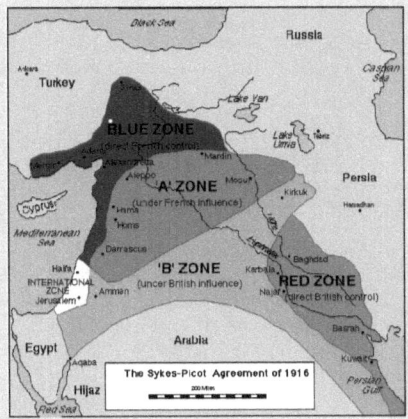

Figure 4 Sykes-Picot Agreement carves up Middle-East

This Judeo-Christian alliance is what has brought the "European, white-Jews" the land in which they currently occupy by agreement. As a result the Balfour Declaration and the Sykes-Picot Agreements had reshaped the borderless lands of the middle-east.

According to the agreement, France was to exercise direct control over Cilicia, the coastal strip of Syria, Lebanon and the greater part of Galilee, up to the line stretching from north of Acre to the northwest corner of the Sea of Galilee (**"Blue Zone"**). Eastward, in the Syrian hinterland, an Arab state was to be created under French protection (**"Area A"**). Britain was to exercise control over southern Mesopotamia (**"Red Zone"**), as well as the territory around the Acre-Haifa bay in the Mediterranean with rights to build a railway from there to Baghdad. The territory east of the Jordan River and the Negev desert, south of the line stretching from Gaza to the Dead Sea, was allocated to an Arab state under British protection (**"Area B"**). South of France's "blue zone," in the area covering the Sanjak of Jerusalem and extending southwards toward the line running approximately from Gaza to the Dead Sea, was to be under international administration (**"Brown Zone"**).

Jerry Falwell, Pat Robertson, John Hague, Jack Van Empe, Creflo Dollar, Bishop Butler and dozens more like them have built their mega sized ministries by promoting Israel as a political state and the Jews as a chosen race... Thousands of local church leaders are following this example. They are the Pharisees of today...

A marketing plan by Touch Point Solutions, a Colorado Springs consulting agency hired by Israel's Ministry of Tourism, describes how to appeal to U.S. evangelicals.

Highlights include:

Persuading the top 30 evangelical Zionists, through face-to-face meetings, to visit and promote Israel. Those named in a separate Touch- Point document, "Who are the Christian Zionists?" include religious broadcaster Jerry Falwell, Christian Coalition founder Pat Robertson, Texas pastor John Hagee, best-selling author Tim LaHaye. Sending a letter to the 100,000 largest evangelical churches and a postcard to

350,000 others, directing them to Israel's tourism Web site, {www.Golsrael.com}; Conducting "Israel Solidarity Days" in 100 cities... Public prayer ceremonies will focus on Israel and its biblical importance. Privately, local evangelical leaders — whether pastors, business people or athletes — will be urged to make "solidarity trips" to Israel in which some will have their expenses paid in full by Israel. (Enterprise, 1916).

Realistically, these ties go back to the crusades and are today re-emerging. Busch Jr. himself mentioned that his invasion into Iraq was something that "god" told him to do bringing their religious base to the framework of the agenda. What people need to realize is at the base of this alliance is Zionism and Zion-ism is Satanic...

Falsehood has many variations and many faces, but truth is absolute...but through subtle manipulations this obvious principal has literally been flipped on end with truth having many paths and falsehood is whatever opposes. Without knowledge the human being would be subjugated to desires and philosophies of many kinds being lead blindly to what appeals thus giving these grouping a mission statement of orientation to their targeted individuals. The Prophet Muhammad s.a.w. said, "seeking knowledge is obligator on every man, woman & child above the age of maturity"...he further said, "When Allah wants good for a person he makes him/her understand his religion." [Sahih Bukhari].

Muhammad s.a.w. In the Bible

For those of us over the age of 40 may recall the red-letter bibles which highlighted in red the words regarded to Jesus...in addition one might even remember when the word "Ahmad" still appeared in the bible as I do. Grandson to an Ol'school minister, I heard my grandfather speak and regarded Eesa ibn Mariam a.s. (Jesus) as a prophet who was born of miraculous conditions, but he also prophesied about the one who would come after him which today is most regarded to as the "comforter".

الَّذِينَ يَتَّبِعُونَ الرَّسُولَ النَّبِيَّ الأُمِّيَّ الَّذِي يَجِدُونَهُ مَكْتُوبًا عِندَهُمْ فِي التَّوْرَاةِ وَالإِنجِيلِ يَأْمُرُهُم بِالْمَعْرُوفِ وَيَنْهَاهُمْ عَنِ الْمُنكَرِ وَيُحِلُّ لَهُمُ الطَّيِّبَاتِ وَيُحَرِّمُ عَلَيْهِمُ الْخَبَائِثَ وَيَضَعُ عَنْهُمْ إِصْرَهُمْ وَالأَغْلاَلَ الَّتِي كَانَتْ عَلَيْهِمْ ۚ فَالَّذِينَ آمَنُوا بِهِ وَعَزَّرُوهُ وَنَصَرُوهُ وَاتَّبَعُوا النُّورَ الَّذِي أُنزِلَ مَعَهُ ۙ أُولَٰئِكَ هُمُ الْمُفْلِحُونَ

Those who follow the Messenger, the unlettered prophet, whom they find written in what they have of the Torah and the Gospel, who enjoins upon them what is right and forbids them what is wrong and makes lawful for them the good things and prohibits for them the evil and relieves them of their burden and the shackles which were upon them. So they who have believed in him, honored him, supported him and followed the light which was sent down with him - it is those who will be the successful. [Al-Araf 7:157]

قُلْ يَا أَيُّهَا النَّاسُ إِنِّي رَسُولُ اللَّهِ إِلَيْكُمْ جَمِيعًا الَّذِي لَهُ مُلْكُ السَّمَاوَاتِ وَالْأَرْضِ لَا إِلَٰهَ إِلَّا هُوَ يُحْيِي وَيُمِيتُ فَآمِنُوا بِاللَّهِ وَرَسُولِهِ النَّبِيِّ الْأُمِّيِّ الَّذِي يُؤْمِنُ بِاللَّهِ وَكَلِمَاتِهِ وَاتَّبِعُوهُ لَعَلَّكُمْ تَهْتَدُونَ

Say, [O Muhammad], "O mankind, indeed I am the Messenger of Allah to you all, [from Him] to whom belongs the dominion of the heavens and the earth. There is no deity except Him; He gives life and causes death." So believe in Allah and His Messenger, the unlettered prophet, who believes in Allah and His words, and follow him that you may be guided. [Al-Araf 7:158]

It is mentioned in the book of Isaiah chapter 29 verse 12:

"And the book is delivered to him that is not learned, saying, Read this, I pray thee: and he saith, I am not learned."

The recently uncovered Gospels of Barnabus that were found in Istanbul (*Ancient Constantinople, Byzantine Emperor*) and carbon dated back to the time of the disciples has indeed shed light on the manipulation and cover up to this catastrophic deception. However, despite this major finding along with the other missed details of truth that still lie in previous scripture, some people are still convoluted to differ...Go figure!!! Extremely arrogant with baseless argument, it only points to credit the excellence of the brainwashing that has been done often with ethnic-centrism connotations. Indeed, if the world came to a common accord of recognition to this truth, which still lies in previous scripture, now historical scripture recently discovered, and the remaining intact last scripture (Quran); the world might just be able to regain a fair amount of its lost harmony...

Prophet Muhammad (saw) is mentioned by name in the Song of Solomon chapter 5 verse 16: "*Hikko Mamittakim we kullo Muhammadim Zehdoodeh wa Zehraee Bayna Jerusalem.*" "His mouth is most sweet: yea, he is altogether lovely (*loved in Arabic Habibullah another reference used for him*). This is my beloved, and this is my friend, O daughters of Jerusalem." In the Hebrew language "**im**" is added for respect. Similarly "im" is added after the name of Prophet Muhammad (saw) to make it Muhammadim. In English translation they have even translated the name of Prophet Muhammad (saw) as "altogether lovely", but in the Old Testament in Hebrew, the name of Prophet Muhammad (saw) is yet present.

Al-Qur'an Chapter 61 Verse 6:

"And remember, Jesus, the son of Mary, said, 'O Children of Israel! I am the messenger of Allah (sent) to you, confirming the Law (which came) before me and giving glad tidings of a messenger to come after me, whose name shall be Ahmed.' But when he came to them with clear signs, they said, 'This is evident sorcery!' "

1. John chapter 14 verse 16: "And I will pray the Father, and he shall give you another Comforter, that he may abide with you forever."

2. Gospel of John chapter 15 verse 26:
"But when the Comforter is come, whom I will send unto you from the Father, even the Spirit of truth, which proceedeth from the Father, he shall testify of me." {Muhammad s.a.w. is the most important voice to ever confirm Jesus, and his return}

3. Gospel of John chapter 16 verse 7:
"Nevertheless I tell you the truth; it is expedient for you that I go away: for if I go not away, the Comforter will not come unto you; but if I depart, I will send him unto you". "Ahmed" or "Muhammad" meaning "the one who praises" or "the praised one" is almost the translation of the Greek word *Periclytos*. In the Gospel of John 14:16, 15:26, and 16:7. The word 'Comforter' is used in the English translation for the Greek word *Paracletos* which means advocate or a kind of friend rather than a comforter. *Paracletos* is the warped reading for *Periclytos*. Jesus (pbuh) actually prophesied Ahmed by name. Even the Greek word *Paraclete* refers to the Prophet (pbuh) who is a mercy for all creatures. Some Christians say that the Comforter mentioned in these prophecies refers to the Holy Spirit. They fail to realize that the prophecy clearly says that only if Jesus (pbuh) departs will the Comforter come. The Bible states that the Holy Spirit was already present on earth before and during the time of Jesus (pbuh), in the womb of Elizabeth, and again when Jesus (pbuh) was being baptized, etc. Hence this prophecy refers to none other than Prophet Muhammad (saw).

4. Gospel of John chapter 16 verse 12-14:
"I have yet many things to say unto you, but ye cannot bear them now. Howbeit when **he**, the Spirit of truth is
come, **he** will guide you unto all truth: for **he** shall not speak of **himself**; but whatsoever **he** shall hear, that shall **he** speak: and **he** will shew you things to come. **He** shall glorify me". [Jesus is mentioned in the Quran more than Muhammad (saw) and Muhammad glorifies Jesus and his return in the end times].
The Spirit of Truth, spoken about in this prophecy refers to none other than Prophet Muhammad (saw) (Swift, Truth over Falsehood, 2016).

Further Clarity about the use and term "Spirit"

The mixture of human reason and bits taken from the bible and other sources deludes the truth about the soul even further, and only serves to open the door for a succession of non-conclusive ideas about its truth. The soul is an element or branch of knowledge that the creator has shared only a little bit of Knowledge about:

وَيَسْأَلُونَكَ عَنِ الرُّوحِ قُلِ الرُّوحُ مِنْ أَمْرِ رَبِّي وَمَا أُوتِيتُم مِّن الْعِلْمِ إِلاَّ قَلِيلاً

And they ask you (O Muhammad SAW) concerning the Ruh (the Spirit); Say: "The Ruh (the Spirit): it is one of the things, the knowledge of which is only with my Lord. And of knowledge, you (mankind) have been given only a little." [Surah Al-Isra 17:85}

The Soul/Spirit is termed Ruh (rooh) in Arabic and this is the element from the creator which is pure. A particular proof of that would be "the breathe" of the creator was blown onto Adam in which Adam them became a human being (meaning alive with conscious). However, the term Ruh is used in other ways such as to refer to the Angel Jabril a.s. (Gabriel), who is Allah's messenger of revelation of whom the prophets would see etc. In the bible the English translation is used "spirit". The best example would be *John 16:13 But when he, the Spirit of truth, comes, he will guide you into all the truth. He will not speak on his own; he will speak only what he hears, and he will tell you what is yet to come.*
If you remember what I said about the term Ruh/Spirit is used when referring to the purity of something, so in the case of the bible the term spirit was referring to the prophet that was to come after Eesa bin Mariam a.s. (Jesus) who was the one speaking in that verse. Now, many Christians have translated that word spirit to mean the only ghost or comforter as some put it...but i invite you to watch the short series i prepared on that particular topic.

So, the use of the term is used to refer to purity i.e. Angels, and the nature/character of prophets who were of the creators chosen people (most pure of people) to deliver his message. But, the Ruh most commonly refers to the Ruh/Spirit while it is still without the body.... The body made of clay & all the soils of the earth that depict all the various ethnicity, texture, and characteristics it produces; is inclined to lowly desires while the spirit is inclined to higher spiritual purpose. This is the fundamental difference between the soul and the Ruh/spirit. The soul is a term that in fact resembles the definition of the self-merged with the spirit which now has a conscious....Effectively the "SELF"...

So, having differences of inclination we can further define these particular aspects of the "Nafs"...

1. An-Nafs Al-ammarah (which means the self, and ammarah comes from the word Amr which means command) thus this stage of the Nafs/self is more so compelled by its desires which either physiological or psychological needs or drives will encourage it towards meeting those needs. Hence the need for knowledge, knowledge and the ability to reason in gaining knowledge sets the human being apart from the animal kingdom. However, without knowledge the human being will live a life of just seeking to fulfill his/her desires and never surpasses this stage. {Quran 12:53}
2. An-Nafs Al-lawwamah (which means the self, and lawwamah comes from lawm which means reproach, admonition, censure, rebuke) this stage comes with the gathering of some knowledge in which the do and don'ts of life are understood. If actions are done that are wrong, this stage of the self feels regret and the definitions mentioned now come into play in admonishing the self towards seeking forgiveness and leaving off repeating those bad actions. {Quran 75:2}
3. An-nafs Al-mutma'innah (which means the self, and mutma'innah means reassured, tranquil, calm, unconcerned, safe, secure) this is the stage that we are meant to strive for and it's the highest level of worldly life one can reach. This is a stage of full self-actualization through recognition of who the creator is and through employing all the knowledge of this truth, we become free from the shackles of worldly life and therefor transcend to higher spiritual states while still in the physical world. The descriptions of the word are the characteristics of those we see who have reached an inner peace with contentment despite worldly status... {Quran 89:27-28}

Therefore it is upon each and every one of us to strive in this life, for that is the true purpose and the only action suitable towards acceptance into the paradise of eternal life. Appetites and desires are the conditions placed upon us that will remain the forces that try to mislead us {Quran 7:176}. Doubts and garbled up truth {Quran 91:7-10} and outline the path that leads to the winners circle. It is thereby through good deeds that sustain the Self/Nafs in a pure state of equilibrium. (Swift, Motivations , 2015)

Fitrah (natural human disposition)

As in previous ages of generations that have preceded us, many people have fallen victim to the incorrect assumption of the heredity of religious truth & practice. Deviation from monotheism to secular views has been a consistent re-invention of evil in every age hence the continuance of guidance to mankind from the creator with prophets ending with Muhammad s.a.w.

وَوَصَّيْنَا الْإِنسَانَ بِوَالِدَيْهِ حَمَلَتْهُ أُمُّهُ وَهْنًا عَلَىٰ وَهْنٍ وَفِصَالُهُ فِي عَامَيْنِ أَنِ اشْكُرْ لِي وَلِوَالِدَيْكَ إِلَيَّ الْمَصِيرُ

And We have enjoined upon man [care] for his parents. His mother carried him, [increasing her] in weakness upon weakness, and his weaning is in two years. Be grateful to Me and to your parents; to Me is the [final] destination. [Al-Luqman 31:14]

وَإِن جَاهَدَاكَ عَلَىٰ أَن تُشْرِكَ بِي مَا لَيْسَ لَكَ بِهِ عِلْمٌ فَلَا تُطِعْهُمَا وَصَاحِبْهُمَا فِي الدُّنْيَا مَعْرُوفًا وَاتَّبِعْ سَبِيلَ مَنْ أَنَابَ إِلَيَّ ثُمَّ إِلَيَّ مَرْجِعُكُمْ فَأُنَبِّئُكُم بِمَا كُنتُمْ تَعْمَلُونَ

But if they endeavor to make you associate with Me that of which you have no knowledge, do not obey them but accompany them in [this] world with appropriate kindness and follow the way of those who turn back to Me [in repentance]. Then to Me will be your return, and I will inform you about what you used to do. [Al-Luqman 31:15]

وَإِذْ أَخَذَ رَبُّكَ مِن بَنِي آدَمَ مِن ظُهُورِهِمْ ذُرِّيَّتَهُمْ وَأَشْهَدَهُمْ عَلَىٰ أَنفُسِهِمْ أَلَسْتُ بِرَبِّكُمْ قَالُوا بَلَىٰ شَهِدْنَا أَن تَقُولُوا يَوْمَ الْقِيَامَةِ إِنَّا كُنَّا عَنْ هَٰذَا غَافِلِينَ

And [mention] when your Lord took from the children of Adam - from their loins - their descendants and made them testify of themselves, [saying to them], "Am I not your Lord?" They said, "Yes, we have testified." [This] - Lest you should say on the day of Resurrection, "Indeed, we were of this unaware." [Al-Ar'raf 7:172]

أَوْ تَقُولُوا إِنَّمَا أَشْرَكَ آبَاؤُنَا مِن قَبْلُ وَكُنَّا ذُرِّيَّةً مِّن بَعْدِهِمْ أَفَتُهْلِكُنَا بِمَا فَعَلَ الْمُبْطِلُونَ

Or [lest] you say, "It was only that our fathers associated [others in worship] with Allah before, and we were but descendants after them. Then would you destroy us for what the falsifiers have done?" [Al-Ar'raf 7:173]

Allah then explained why He had all of mankind bear witness that He is their creator and only true God worthy of worship. He said, "That was In case you (mankind) should say on the day of Resurrection, "Verily we were unaware of all this." That is to say, we had no idea that You Allah, were our God. No one told us that we were only supposed to worship you alone. Allah went on to explain that it was also In case you should say, "Certainly It was our ancestors who made partners (With Allah) and we are only their descendants; will you then destroy us for what those liars did?" Thus, every child is born with a natural belief in Allah and an inborn inclination to worship Him alone called in Arabic "Fitrah".

If the child were left alone, he would worship Allah in his own way, but all children are affected by those things around them, seen or unseen.

The Prophet (PEUH) reported that Allah said, "I created my servants in the right religion but devils made them go astray". The Prophet (PBUH) also said, "Each child is born in a state of "Fitrah"{natural human disposition to monotheism}, then his parents make him/her a Jew, Christian or a Zoroastrian..., look to the way an animal gives birth to a normal offspring; Have you noticed any that were born mutilated?" (Collected by Bukhari and Muslim).

So, just as the child submits to the physical laws which Allah has put in nature, his soul also submits naturally to the fact that Allah is his Lord and Creator. But, his parents try to make him follow their own way and the child is not strong enough in the early stages of his life to resist or oppose the will of his parents. The religion which the child follows at this stage is one of custom and upbringing and Allah does not hold him to account or punish him for this religion or way of the parents (By Abu Ameena Bilal Phillips); however, there comes a time in everyone's life when the truth is re-presented to us when we have gained maturity and it is now on us that we choose to keep a course derailed from our nature or regain its harmony. We all have been given individually eyes, ears, and faculty as well as capacity of intellect to contemplate for ourselves therefore blind following is evil and detested. This is the importance of personal acquisition of true knowledge...For the thousands who continue to enter Islam it is the fulfilling aspect of its knowledge that satisfies & reintroduces lost souls with their natural link and this is the over-whelming aspect that conquerors many into submission & love of what they undoubtedly recognize as the truth...

Elohim El, Elah, Alah
In the Bible, God is very often referred to as 'Elohim' in the Hebrew language. The 'im' in the ending is a plural of honour and God is referred to as 'El' or 'Elah' in the English Bible with commentary, edited by reverend C. I. Scofield. 'Elah' is alternatively spelled as 'Alah'. The difference in spelling is only of a single 'L'. Muslims spell Allah as 'Allah' while the Reverend has spelled it as Alah and they pronounce it as 'Elah'. Muslims pronounce it as Allah. Hebrew and Arabic are sister languages therefore we say it should be pronounced as 'Allah' and not as 'Elah'.

When I was in school, I was taught 'D, O' is do, 'T, O' is to. What is 'G, O' It is 'go' and not 'gu'. 'N, U, T' is nut, 'C, U, T' cut; 'B, U, T' is but, what is 'P, U, T'? Not 'pat' but it is 'put'. If you ask "Why?" The answer is "It is their language". If I have to pass I have to say 'P, U, T' is 'put' and not 'pat'. Similarly the right pronunciation for A, L, L, A, H, is Allah...

Jesus (pbuh) cried out Allah Allah when he was put on the cross It is
mentioned in the New Testament in the Gospel of Mathew, chapter 27 verse 46 as well as Gospel of Mark, chapter 15 verse 34 when Jesus (pbuh) was put on the cross.

> Jesus cried with a loud voice saying "E'-Li, E'-Li la'-ma sa-bach'-tha-ni?" that is to say, 'My God, My God why hast Thou Forsaken Me?' Does this sound like Jehovah! Jehovah! Why have thou forsaken me? Does it sound like *Abba Abba*? The answer is 'No'. Hebrew and Arabic are sister languages and if you translate "E'-Li, E'-Li la'-ma sa-bach'-tha-ni" into Arabic it is 'Allah Allah *lama tarak tani*' does it sound similar?

> This statement of Jesus (pbuh), "E'-Li, E'-Li la'-ma sa-bach'-tha-ni" is preserved in its original Hebrew in each and every of its translation which is available in more than 2000 different languages of the world and in each and every of them, "Allah" is present.

"Allah" in Sikhism
one of the names by which Gurunanak Sahib referred to God is "Allah".

"Allah" in Hinduism

    a. **"Allah" in Rigveda Book 2 Hymn I verse II**
        Even in the Rigveda which is the most sacred scripture of the Hindus, one
        of the attributes given to God Almighty in Book no 2 Hymn no I verse II, is
        '*Ila*' which if pronounced properly is the same as Allah.

    b. **Allo Upanishad:**
        Amongst the various Upanishads one of the Upanishad is named as '*Allo*'
        Upanishad in which God is referred to as "Allah" several times. **(Naik)**

Social Psychology

Aspects of human social behaviors and other motivating factors have been peered into
as a result to better understanding ourselves & our interactions. For example
altruism...the selfless act done solely for the benefit of someone else not expecting any
return of favor. This particular action is one of the marks of characteristics for a believer
since the Prophet s.a.w said, "None truly believes until he/she wants for their
brother/sister what they want for themselves." Brother/sister here denotes society as we
are all human and by that seen as family...

يُوفُونَ بِالنَّذْرِ وَيَخَافُونَ يَوْمًا كَانَ شَرُّهُ مُسْتَطِيرًا

They [are those who] fulfill [their] vows and fear a Day whose evil will be
widespread.[Al-Insan 76;7]
وَيُطْعِمُونَ الطَّعَامَ عَلَى حُبِّهِ مِسْكِينًا وَيَتِيمًا وَأَسِيرًا

And they give food in spite of love for it to the needy, the orphan, and the captive, [Al-
Insan 76:8]
إِنَّمَا نُطْعِمُكُمْ لِوَجْهِ اللَّهِ لَا نُرِيدُ مِنكُمْ جَزَاءً وَلَا شُكُورًا

[Saying], "We feed you only for the countenance of Allah. We wish not from you reward
or gratitude. [Al-Insan 76:9]

الَّذِي يُؤْتِي مَالَهُ يَتَزَكَّىٰ

[He] who gives [from] his wealth to purify himself [Al-Lail 98:18]

وَمَا لِأَحَدٍ عِندَهُ مِن نِّعْمَةٍ تُجْزَىٰ

And not [giving] for anyone who has [done him] a favor to be rewarded [Al-Lail 98:19]

إِلَّا ابْتِغَاءَ وَجْهِ رَبِّهِ الْأَعْلَىٰ

But only seeking the countenance of his Lord, Most High. [Al-Lail 98:20]

Empathy towards others is something that has definitely fallen victim to de-humanizing agents. So, what is the recognition and means by which we want to help each other today?
- Is it because it's a woman?
- Because there is no one around?
- Or because we just witnessed someone else helping and we feel obligated?
- Maybe someone appears to be in need?
- We're not in a hurry
- We're in a good mood
- Or the needy is similar to us in some way

Whatever the case me be...we understand these characteristics are most apparent in those who are god fearing (Al-muta'qoon), those who are immune to societal views and have far stronger religious ties that instill empathetic views for our fellow man despite our differences.

If man were to come into being by accident or by sheer chance, his entire life would be based on chance, and his whole existence would be meaningless. But no sensible man can conceive of his life as meaningless, and no rational being would leave his existence at the mercy of fluctuating chance. Every reasonable human being tries to make his life as meaningful as possible and set for himself a model of conduct according to some design. Individuals, groups and nations do plan their course of action, and every careful plan produces some desired effects through a collective world view through learned beliefs, values, and religious traditions (in secular view). Thus it has become more inherently the ideals of secular culture that has redrawn its own behavior much of which is apparently harmful with worsening trajectory, but in addition it also seeks to carbon copy these same behaviors around the world in export.

One thing about secularism is it continues to fractionalize into smaller and smaller groups...the collective society turns to individualism, and then from individualism grouping based on common desires, drives, and thoughts... beliefs arise that are used to achieve the goals of that the group for individual benefit because we can by ourselves achieve nothing. Individualism is something that is dominant in the United States, while in South America, Africa and Asia it is collectivism that is dominant in culture.

Collective cultures understand and value the importance of the group, tribe, community; Nation...Individual benefit is a by-product of the collective whole and can never be otherwise.

Television as a Weapon

Subconscious manipulation is something people need to be aware of and more importantly how it works. What the conscious mind believes the subconscious mind acts on...Very similar to the programming of the computer (*the reasons for introducing our similarities to the computer earlier*), information is fed into a computer via keyboard or other peripheral devices as do the senses of the human being; however no matter the integrity of the information, the computer will still act on the information it is fed. Likewise, if a person believes something that is not true the memory banks of the subconscious mind do not correct the error, but instead act on it. The theory of cognitive dissonance holds that a mind automatically & involuntary rejects information not in line with previous accepted thoughts, behavior & beliefs.

Unaware by most and in recognition of those who seek to manipulate now that watching television alters the state of consciousness. Bypassing the top layer of consciousness by sound & visual patterns that are produced, which can unperceivably change brain wave patterns from consciousness to subconscious states. By controlling the delivery of the programming speed, tone, visual aids, it produces hypnotic type qualities that can very easy take hold of the individual. The acceptance of the material now depends on two things: the source (if it's a trusted source) and repetition (which is why you see news sources always repeating the information around the clock). Most people think news source are reputable, therefore they focus on repetition of the material to manipulate its following. Trusting the source creates acceptance of the information even it's not true or not fully understood. Repetition of the information paired with the trusted source is merely a conditioned stimulus paired to a known neutral stimulus in order to bring about a conditioned response...This is known as learned behavior, and once the neutral stimulus becomes the condition by which the conditioned response takes place the behavior has now been effectively altered.

It's fair to say that what is missed consciously in meant for the subconscious...In the 1960's a scientist who worked for General Electric {experiments conducted by researcher Herbert Krugman} discovered that within 30sec to a min a person's brain goes from a beta wave state {alert, awake, primary left brain cognition} to an alpha wave state {relaxed, day-dreaming, right hemisphere} where a person basically goes on auto-pilot. This condition is observable when a person gets a sort of glazed looked over their face, or an open, dropped lower lip with children. Also their inability to hear when called, because of this alteration in consciousness. In this state one becomes a passive learner to the information that is fed to him/her. In conversation with someone that watches a lot of television you'll recognize the shallowness of the insight into topics, lack of spark of their own opinions from contemplation/ deep thought & repeated television type answers. That's' because in this passive state the information can't be critically analyzed & it is therefore fed directly into the subconscious state for programming purposes only. From these experiments they were able to see that television was a form of mind control. The word "addiction" usually refers to a psychological or physical dependence on a particular experience that must be repeated in order for a person to be comfortable. Usually, we think about this in terms of chemical addiction, which occurs when the addict's chemical of choice reorganizes the nervous system so that it requires the presence of that chemical to operate smoothly returning the person to a state of homeostasis. But any behavior that is pleasurable will lead to an experience that will require its repetition especially if the acquisition requires very little work. This small detail is what psychologist call positive reinforcement which brings its incentive to repeat the behavior etc. Media consumption (all forms of media) on average is around 15.5 hrs/day as of 2015. More sinister yet, the mass media has built their programming around special times of the day to feed these programs to the public in helping to restructure cognition of television viewers. 1980's and 90's T.V. sitcoms were extremely popular in restructuring those generation in their attitudes, trends, acceptable social behavior, and even more importantly the family aspect. We are able to see all of these subtle but drastic changes within our society like different layers of distinction within each one.

"The conscious and intelligent manipulation of organized habits and opinions of the masses is an important element in a democratic society. Those who manipulate this unseen mechanism of society constitute an invisible government which is the true ruling power in our country."

—Edward Bernays "propaganda" 1928 (Moore, 2001)

What Mr. Bernays is quoted in saying is very important for people to reconsider. It literally blows my mind that most people today are completely brainwashed as to what Democracy really is and what it meant to those who constructed the United States Constitution...Democracy is something that is individual based, giving individuality to even the unborn child (*which has its rights to life, but shouldn't be considered into the majority voice in politics choosing their side by unlawful proxy of partisanship*). Therefore it seeks to solidify the people on common opinion, thought, belief etc.... This grouping depict either majority or minority by which the majority has the democratic right over the minority. Even if the majority are immorally wrong in act, thought, or belief; their democratic authority of majority will supersede all others and the individuals of the minority have no rights. Therefore, manipulation to shifts ideals and circumstances is the invisible hand in shaping the majority to their practices and gaining "Mob-Rule."

*"Let the American youth never forget that they possess a noble inheritance, bought by the toils and sufferings and blood of their ancestors, and capable, if wisely improved and faithfully guarded, of transmitting to the latest posterity all the substantial blessings of life, the peaceful enjoyment of liberty, property, religion, and independence. The structure has been erected by architects of consummate skill and fidelity; its foundations are solid, its compartments are beautiful as well as useful, its arrangements are full of wisdom and order, and its defenses are impregnable from without. It has been reared for immortality, if the work of men may justly aspire to such a title. **It may nevertheless perish in an hour by the folly, or corruption, or negligence of its only keepers, the People.** Republics are created by the virtue, public spirit, and intelligence of the citizens. **They fall when the wise are banished from the public councils because they dare to be honest, and the profligate are rewarded because they flatter the people in order to betray them."***

— Joseph Story (1779-1845) Lawyer, Supreme Court Justice & influential commentators on the U.S. Constitution

"Democracy will soon degenerate into an anarchy; such an anarchy that every man will do what is right in his own eyes and no man's life or property or reputation or liberty will be secure, and every one of these will soon mould itself into a system of subordination of all the moral virtues and intellectual abilities, all the powers of wealth, beauty, wit, and science, to the wanton pleasures, the capricious will, and the execrable [abominable] cruelty of one or a very few."

— John Adams (1797-1801) Second President of the United States and Patriot (Swift, Country or Corporation, 2015)

Hypnotic states should then be understood to be states of mind that lack self-critique self-analysis and becoming a state of mind that has shifted towards suggestion...

Islam agrees with Western psychologist Correction

Social psychologist Robert Cialdini list some key points he believes are critical to instill within people and children in an effort to counter the effects of manipulation within society that are undoing its cohesion and ability to sustain itself. Most of his suggestions are exactly what Islam calls to in the protection of the individual, community, and environment.

Teaching children to disobey *unjust* authority

يَا أَيُّهَا الَّذِينَ آمَنُوا أَطِيعُوا اللَّهَ وَأَطِيعُوا الرَّسُولَ وَأُولِي الْأَمْرِ مِنكُمْ ۖ فَإِن تَنَازَعْتُمْ فِي شَيْءٍ فَرُدُّوهُ إِلَى اللَّهِ وَالرَّسُولِ إِن كُنتُمْ تُؤْمِنُونَ بِاللَّهِ وَالْيَوْمِ الْآخِرِ ۚ ذَٰلِكَ خَيْرٌ وَأَحْسَنُ تَأْوِيلًا

O you who have believed, obey Allah and obey the Messenger and those in authority among you. And if you disagree over anything, refer it to Allah and the Messenger {meaning to the Quran and the Sunnah of the Prophet for answer}, if you should believe in Allah and the Last Day. That is the best [way] and best in result. [An-Nisa 4:59]

هُوَ اللَّهُ الَّذِي لَا إِلَٰهَ إِلَّا هُوَ ۖ عَالِمُ الْغَيْبِ وَالشَّهَادَةِ ۖ هُوَ الرَّحْمَٰنُ الرَّحِيمُ

He is Allah, other than whom there is no deity, Knower of the unseen and the witnessed. He is the Entirely Merciful, the Especially Merciful. [Al-Hashr 59:22]

هُوَ اللَّهُ الَّذِي لَا إِلَٰهَ إِلَّا هُوَ الْمَلِكُ الْقُدُّوسُ السَّلَامُ الْمُؤْمِنُ الْمُهَيْمِنُ الْعَزِيزُ الْجَبَّارُ الْمُتَكَبِّرُ ۚ سُبْحَانَ اللَّهِ عَمَّا يُشْرِكُونَ

He is Allah, other than whom there is no deity, the Sovereign, the Pure, the Perfection, the Bestower of Faith, the Overseer, the Exalted in Might, the Compeller, the Superior. Exalted is Allah above whatever they associate with Him. [Al-Hashr 59:23]

هُوَ اللَّهُ الْخَالِقُ الْبَارِئُ الْمُصَوِّرُ ۖ لَهُ الْأَسْمَاءُ الْحُسْنَىٰ ۚ يُسَبِّحُ لَهُ مَا فِي السَّمَاوَاتِ وَالْأَرْضِ ۖ وَهُوَ الْعَزِيزُ الْحَكِيمُ

He is Allah, the Creator, the Inventor, the Fashioner; to Him belong the best names. Whatever is in the heavens and earth is exalting Him. And He is the Exalted in Might, the Wise. [Al-Hashr 59:24]

Beginning with the supreme authority we should instill the knowledge of Allah in our children. In recognition that Allah is first in everything and without his authority there is no authority and no being...

Support critical thinking abilities in children – asking for support of assertions, separation of rhetoric and conclusion, developing means vs. ends thinking

أَفَمَن يَمْشِي مُكِبًّا عَلَىٰ وَجْهِهِ أَهْدَىٰ أَمَّن يَمْشِي سَوِيًّا عَلَىٰ صِرَاطٍ مُّسْتَقِيمٍ

Then is one who walks fallen on his face better guided or one who walks erect on a straight path? [Al-Mulk 67:22]

قُلۡ هُوَ الَّذِي أَنشَأَكُمۡ وَجَعَلَ لَكُمُ السَّمۡعَ وَالۡأَبۡصَارَ وَالۡأَفۡئِدَةَ ۖ قَلِيلًا مَّا تَشۡكُرُونَ

Say, "It is He who has produced you and made for you hearing and vision and hearts; little are you grateful."[Al-Mulk 67:23]

Rewarding social modeling of moral behavior

قُلۡ آمَنَّا بِاللَّهِ وَمَا أُنزِلَ عَلَيۡنَا وَمَا أُنزِلَ عَلَىٰ إِبۡرَاهِيمَ وَإِسۡمَاعِيلَ وَإِسۡحَاقَ وَيَعۡقُوبَ وَالۡأَسۡبَاطِ وَمَا أُوتِيَ مُوسَىٰ وَعِيسَىٰ وَالنَّبِيُّونَ مِن رَّبِّهِمۡ لَا نُفَرِّقُ بَيۡنَ أَحَدٍ مِّنۡهُمۡ وَنَحۡنُ لَهُ مُسۡلِمُونَ

Say, "We have believed in Allah and in what was revealed to us and what was revealed to Abraham, Ishmael, Isaac, Jacob, and the Descendants, and in what was given to Moses and Jesus and to the prophets from their Lord. We make no distinction between any of them, and we are Muslims [submitting] to Him." [Al-Imran 3:84]

لَّقَدۡ كَانَ لَكُمۡ فِي رَسُولِ اللَّهِ أُسۡوَةٌ حَسَنَةٌ لِّمَن كَانَ يَرۡجُو اللَّهَ وَالۡيَوۡمَ الۡآخِرَ وَذَكَرَ اللَّهَ كَثِيرًا

There has certainly been for you in the Messenger of Allah an excellent pattern for anyone whose hope is in Allah and the Last Day and [who] remembers Allah often.[Al-Azhab 33:21]

We have the best example in the Prophet s.a.w. and the best examples in his wives and the blessed mother of Eesa ibn Mariam a.s. {Mariam bint Imran a.s.}

Social recognition for good deeds; acknowledging the bravery of whistleblowers of misconduct

وَلۡتَكُن مِّنكُمۡ أُمَّةٌ يَدۡعُونَ إِلَى الۡخَيۡرِ وَيَأۡمُرُونَ بِالۡمَعۡرُوفِ وَيَنۡهَوۡنَ عَنِ الۡمُنكَرِ ۚ وَأُولَٰئِكَ هُمُ الۡمُفۡلِحُونَ

And let there be [arising] from you a nation inviting to [all that is] good, enjoining what is right and forbidding what is wrong, and those will be the successful.[Al-Imran 3:104]

Promoting critical thinking that challenges false ideologies

Not living on mindless "auto-pilot"

- o Reflect on details of the immediate situation; think before acting out in opposition, investigate matters for their truth.

وَقَالَتِ الۡيَهُودُ لَيۡسَتِ النَّصَارَىٰ عَلَىٰ شَيۡءٍ وَقَالَتِ النَّصَارَىٰ لَيۡسَتِ الۡيَهُودُ عَلَىٰ شَيۡءٍ وَهُمۡ يَتۡلُونَ الۡكِتَابَ ۗ كَذَٰلِكَ قَالَ الَّذِينَ لَا يَعۡلَمُونَ مِثۡلَ قَوۡلِهِمۡ ۚ فَاللَّهُ يَحۡكُمُ بَيۡنَهُمۡ يَوۡمَ الۡقِيَامَةِ فِيمَا كَانُوا فِيهِ يَخۡتَلِفُونَ

The Jews say "The Christians have nothing [true] to stand on," and the Christians say, "The Jews have nothing to stand on," although they [both] recite the Scripture. Thus the polytheists speak the same as their words. But Allah will judge between them on the Day of Resurrection concerning that over which they used to differ.[Al-Baqarah 2:113]

وَقَالُوا كُونُوا هُودًا أَوْ نَصَارَىٰ تَهْتَدُوا ۚ قُلْ بَلْ مِلَّةَ إِبْرَاهِيمَ حَنِيفًا ۖ وَمَا كَانَ مِنَ الْمُشْرِكِينَ

They say, "Be Jews or Christians [so] you will be guided." Say, "Rather, [we follow] the religion of Abraham, inclining toward truth, and he was not of the polytheists."[Al-Baqarah 2:135]

قُولُوا آمَنَّا بِاللَّهِ وَمَا أُنزِلَ إِلَيْنَا وَمَا أُنزِلَ إِلَىٰ إِبْرَاهِيمَ وَإِسْمَاعِيلَ وَإِسْحَاقَ وَيَعْقُوبَ وَالْأَسْبَاطِ وَمَا أُوتِيَ مُوسَىٰ وَعِيسَىٰ وَمَا أُوتِيَ النَّبِيُّونَ مِن رَّبِّهِمْ لَا نُفَرِّقُ بَيْنَ أَحَدٍ مِّنْهُمْ وَنَحْنُ لَهُ مُسْلِمُونَ

Say, [O believers], "We have believed in Allah and what has been revealed to us and what has been revealed to Abraham and Ishmael and Isaac and Jacob and the Descendants and what was given to Moses and Jesus and what was given to the prophets from their Lord. We make no distinction between any of them, and we are Muslims [in submission] to Him."[Al-Baqarah 2:136]

أَمْ تَقُولُونَ إِنَّ إِبْرَاهِيمَ وَإِسْمَاعِيلَ وَإِسْحَاقَ وَيَعْقُوبَ وَالْأَسْبَاطَ كَانُوا هُودًا أَوْ نَصَارَىٰ ۗ قُلْ أَأَنتُمْ أَعْلَمُ أَمِ اللَّهُ ۗ وَمَنْ أَظْلَمُ مِمَّن كَتَمَ شَهَادَةً عِندَهُ مِنَ اللَّهِ ۗ وَمَا اللَّهُ بِغَافِلٍ عَمَّا تَعْمَلُونَ

Or do you say that Abraham and Ishmael and Isaac and Jacob and the Descendants were Jews or Christians? Say, "Are you more knowing or is Allah?" And who is more unjust than one who conceals a testimony he has from Allah? And Allah is not unaware of what you do.[Al-Baqarah 2:140]

Encouraging respect for human diversity and appreciating human variability

- o Reduces in-group biases and discrimination

    Not allowing stereotyping and dehumanization of other people

يَا أَيُّهَا النَّاسُ إِنَّا خَلَقْنَاكُم مِّن ذَكَرٍ وَأُنثَىٰ وَجَعَلْنَاكُمْ شُعُوبًا وَقَبَائِلَ لِتَعَارَفُوا ۚ إِنَّ أَكْرَمَكُمْ عِندَ اللَّهِ أَتْقَاكُمْ ۚ إِنَّ اللَّهَ عَلِيمٌ خَبِيرٌ

O mankind, indeed We have created you from male and female and made you peoples and tribes that you may know one another. Indeed, the most noble of you in the sight of Allah is the most righteous of you. Indeed, Allah is Knowing and Acquainted.[Al-Hujurat 49:13]

Changing social conditions that make people feel anonymous

- o Support conditions that make people feel special, have sense of personal value and self-worth

وَلَا تُصَعِّرْ خَذَكَ لِلنَّاسِ وَلَا تَمْشِ فِي الْأَرْضِ مَرَحًا ۖ إِنَّ اللَّهَ لَا يُحِبُّ كُلَّ مُخْتَالٍ فَخُورٍ

And do not turn your cheek [in contempt] toward people and do not walk through the earth exultantly. Indeed, Allah does not like everyone self-deluded and boastful.[Al-Luqman 31:18]

مَا أَصَابَ مِن مُّصِيبَةٍ فِي الْأَرْضِ وَلَا فِي أَنفُسِكُمْ إِلَّا فِي كِتَابٍ مِّن قَبْلِ أَن نَّبْرَأَهَا ۚ إِنَّ ذَٰلِكَ عَلَى اللَّهِ يَسِيرٌ

No disaster strikes upon the earth or among yourselves except that it is in a register before We bring it into being - indeed that, for Allah, is easy [Al-Hadid 57:22]

لِّكَيْلَا تَأْسَوْا عَلَىٰ مَا فَاتَكُمْ وَلَا تَفْرَحُوا بِمَا آتَاكُمْ ۗ وَاللَّهُ لَا يُحِبُّ كُلَّ مُخْتَالٍ فَخُورٍ

In order that you not despair over what has eluded you and not exult [in pride] over what He has given you. And Allah does not like everyone self-deluded and boastful [Al-Hadid 57:23].

Encouraging admission of mistakes, accepting error in judgments – to reduce justification for continuing wrong, immoral behavior

- o Reduces need to justify mistakes and to continue wrong or immoral action
- o Undercuts motivation to reduce dissonance by being consistent with a bad decision

وَقَالَ الَّذِينَ اتَّبَعُوا لَوْ أَنَّ لَنَا كَرَّةً فَنَتَبَرَّأَ مِنْهُمْ كَمَا تَبَرَّءُوا مِنَّا ۗ كَذَٰلِكَ يُرِيهِمُ اللَّهُ أَعْمَالَهُمْ حَسَرَاتٍ عَلَيْهِمْ ۖ وَمَا هُم بِخَارِجِينَ مِنَ النَّارِ

Those who followed will say, "If only we had another turn [at worldly life] so we could disassociate ourselves from them as they have disassociated themselves from us." Thus will Allah show them their deeds as regrets upon them. And they are never to emerge from the Fire. [Al-Baqara 2:167]

Promoting personal responsibility and accountability of one's actions

وَلَا تَزِرُ وَازِرَةٌ وِزْرَ أُخْرَىٰ ۚ وَإِن تَدْعُ مُثْقَلَةٌ إِلَىٰ حِمْلِهَا لَا يُحْمَلْ مِنْهُ شَيْءٌ وَلَوْ كَانَ ذَا قُرْبَىٰ ۗ إِنَّمَا تُنذِرُ الَّذِينَ يَخْشَوْنَ رَبَّهُم بِالْغَيْبِ وَأَقَامُوا الصَّلَاةَ ۚ وَمَن تَزَكَّىٰ فَإِنَّمَا يَتَزَكَّىٰ لِنَفْسِهِ ۚ وَإِلَى اللَّهِ الْمَصِيرُ

And no bearer of burdens will bear the burden of another. And if a heavily laden soul calls [another] to [carry some of] its load, nothing of it will be carried, even if he should be a close relative. You can only warn those who fear their Lord unseen and have established prayer. And whoever purifies himself only purifies himself for [the benefit of] his soul. And to Allah is the [final] destination.[Al-Fatir 35:18]

- o Diffused responsibility is a mere disguise for own role in consequences of actions

Supporting independence over group conformity

- o Increasing awareness of when conformity to the group norm is counter-productive and should not be followed
- o Understanding when independence should take precedence despite possible social rejection

وَإِن تُطِعْ أَكْثَرَ مَن فِي الْأَرْضِ يُضِلُّوكَ عَن سَبِيلِ اللَّهِ ۚ إِن يَتَّبِعُونَ إِلَّا الظَّنَّ وَإِنْ هُمْ إِلَّا يَخْرُصُونَ

And if you obey most of those upon the earth, they will mislead you from the way of Allah. They follow not except assumption, and they are not but falsifying.[Al-An'am 6:116]

Reducing poverty, inequities, and entitlements of the privileged

اللَّهُ الَّذِي جَعَلَ لَكُمُ الْأَرْضَ قَرَارًا وَالسَّمَاءَ بِنَاءً وَصَوَّرَكُمْ فَأَحْسَنَ صُوَرَكُمْ وَرَزَقَكُم مِّنَ الطَّيِّبَاتِ ۚ ذَٰلِكُمُ اللَّهُ رَبُّكُمْ ۖ فَتَبَارَكَ اللَّهُ رَبُّ الْعَالَمِينَ

It is Allah who made for you the earth a place of settlement and the sky a ceiling and formed you and perfected your forms and provided you with good things. That is Allah, your Lord; then blessed is Allah, Lord of the worlds.[Al-Ghafir 40:64]

Never sacrificing freedom for promised security

وَمِنَ النَّاسِ مَن يَتَّخِذُ مِن دُونِ اللَّهِ أَندَادًا يُحِبُّونَهُمْ كَحُبِّ اللَّهِ ۖ وَالَّذِينَ آمَنُوا أَشَدُّ حُبًّا لِّلَّهِ ۗ وَلَوْ يَرَى الَّذِينَ ظَلَمُوا إِذْ يَرَوْنَ الْعَذَابَ أَنَّ الْقُوَّةَ لِلَّهِ جَمِيعًا وَأَنَّ اللَّهَ شَدِيدُ الْعَذَابِ

And [yet], among the people are those who take other than Allah as equals [to Him]. They love them as they [should] love Allah. But those who believe are stronger in love for Allah. And if only they who have wronged would consider [that] when they see the punishment, [they will be certain] that all power belongs to Allah and that Allah is severe in punishment.[Al-Baqarah 2:165]

إِذْ تَبَرَّأَ الَّذِينَ اتُّبِعُوا مِنَ الَّذِينَ اتَّبَعُوا وَرَأَوُا الْعَذَابَ وَتَقَطَّعَتْ بِهِمُ الْأَسْبَابُ

[And they should consider that] when those who have been followed disassociate themselves from those who followed [them], and they [all] see the punishment, and cut off from them are the ties [of relationship],[Al-Baqarah 2:166]

وَقَالَ الَّذِينَ اتَّبَعُوا لَوْ أَنَّ لَنَا كَرَّةً فَنَتَبَرَّأَ مِنْهُمْ كَمَا تَبَرَّءُوا مِنَّا ۗ كَذَٰلِكَ يُرِيهِمُ اللَّهُ أَعْمَالَهُمْ حَسَرَاتٍ عَلَيْهِمْ ۖ وَمَا هُم بِخَارِجِينَ مِنَ النَّارِ

Those who followed will say, "If only we had another turn [at worldly life] so we could disassociate ourselves from them as they have disassociated themselves from us." Thus will Allah show them their deeds as regrets upon them. And they are never to emerge from the Fire.[Al-Baqarah 2:167]

- o Bad deal – sacrificing the real and immediate for the distant and elusive; lose control and relinquish power to the already powerful

Discouraging even the smallest of transgressions, cheating, gossiping, lying, teasing, bullying

- o Provides first steps toward more severe behaviors (Zimbardo, 2006)
- o Can harness the subtle power of small steps in Milgram's paradigm to promote positive actions and altruism until one's does uncharacteristically or previously imaginably good deeds.

يَا أَيُّهَا الَّذِينَ آمَنُوا اجْتَنِبُوا كَثِيرًا مِّنَ الظَّنِّ إِنَّ بَعْضَ الظَّنِّ إِثْمٌ ۖ وَلَا تَجَسَّسُوا وَلَا يَغْتَب بَّعْضُكُم بَعْضًا ۚ أَيُحِبُّ أَحَدُكُمْ أَن يَأْكُلَ لَحْمَ أَخِيهِ مَيْتًا فَكَرِهْتُمُوهُ ۚ وَاتَّقُوا اللَّهَ ۚ إِنَّ اللَّهَ تَوَّابٌ رَّحِيمٌ

O you who have believed, avoid much [negative] assumption. Indeed, some assumption is sin. And do not spy or backbite {*talk behind the back*} each other. Would one of you like to eat the flesh of his brother {*a detestable thought and the punishment for the one who does so In the hereafter*} when dead? You would detest it. And fear Allah; indeed, Allah is Accepting of repentance and Merciful.[Al-Hujurat 49:12]

يَا أَيُّهَا الَّذِينَ آمَنُوا اتَّقُوا اللَّهَ وَقُولُوا قَوْلًا سَدِيدًا

O you who have believed, fear Allah and speak words of appropriate justice. [Al-Azhab 33:70]

Perception is the Commodity, so Why do we Conform?

Bibliography

Wikipedia. (n.d.). *Torches of Freedom*. Retrieved from Wikipedia:
    https://en.wikipedia.org/wiki/Torches_of_Freedom

Abraham Brill . (n.d.). Retrieved from Wikipedia : https://en.wikipedia.org/wiki/Abraham_Brill

Carr, W. G. (1958). Present Dangers. In W. g. Carr, *Pawns in the Game* (p. 203). Ontario Canada:
    Federation of Chrisitian Laymen. Retrieved from http://www.jesus-is-
    savior.com/Evils%20in%20Government/Communism/pawnsinthegame.pdf

Carter, S. (1961, April 27). JFK Speech to the American Newspaper Publishers Association . New York
    City, New York, USA .

Corrobated by Dr. Dennis L. Cuddy PhD. (n.d.). *Albert Pike* . Retrieved from
    http://www.biblebelievers.org.au/pike.htm

Enterprise, A.-I. C. (1916). *Pre-State Israel (The Sykes-Picot Agreement)* . Retrieved from Jewish Vitrual
    Library : http://www.jewishvirtuallibrary.org/jsource/History/sykes_pico.html

Hershorin, B. J. (2003). *Expert Law* . Retrieved from The seperation of Church and State: Have We Gone
    To Far? : http://www.expertlaw.com/library/misc/first_amendment.html

McLeod, S. (2009). *Jean Piaget Cognitive Theory* . Retrieved from Simply Psychology:
    http://www.simplypsychology.org/piaget.html

Monferrato, F. B. (2015). *Language Acquisition.*

Moore, W. (2001). The Journal of Cognitive Liberties . *CCLE*, 59-66.

Naik, D. Z. (n.d.). *Islam 101.* Retrieved from Allah in previous scripture :
    http://www.islam101.com/tauheed/Aior.htm

Piaget's Cognitive Development . (n.d.). Retrieved from
    https://www.google.com/search?q=piaget%27s+theory+of+cognitive+development&tbm=isch&
    imgil=6SNmUc8zw3OCMM%253A%253B4CcXc3_WReXMZM%253Bhttp%25253A%25252F%252
    52Fwww.psychologynoteshq.com%25252Fpiagetstheory%25252F&source=iu&pf=m&fir=6SNm
    Uc8zw3OCMM%253A%252C4

Proctor, R. N. (2011, November 22). *The history and discovery of the cigarette-lung cancer link;*
    evidentiary traditions, corporate denial, global toll. Retrieved from Tobacco Control :
    http://tobaccocontrol.bmj.com/content/21/2/87.full

Sunnah.com . (n.d.). Retrieved from The Hadith of the Prophet Muhammad (saw) :
    http://sunnah.com/bukhari/3/3

Perception is the Commodity, so Why do we Conform?

Swift, S. I. (2015). *Country or Corporation*. Retrieved from Truth over Falsehood :
http://sayyarismail.weebly.com/blog-country-or-corporation

Swift, S. I. (2015). *Motivations* . Retrieved from Truth over Falsehood :
http://sayyarismail.weebly.com/blog-motivations

Swift, S. I. (2015). *The Plot* . Retrieved from Truth over Falsehood : http://sayyarismail.weebly.com/the-
plot.html

Swift, S. I. (2016). *Truth over Falsehood*. Retrieved from Bible-Jesus-Christians:
http://sayyarismail.weebly.com/blog-bible-jesus--christians

Zimbardo, P. G. (2006). *Understanding how people turn Evil*. Retrieved from The Lucifer Effect:
http://www.lucifereffect.com/guide_cialdini-intro.htm